LEAVING LAW

HOW OTHERS DID IT &
HOW YOU CAN TOO

BY ADELE BARLOW

To Christian Barlow and Katherine McDonald,
for bringing this book off my laptop and into the world.

Dream of making partner at your law firm? If so, then this book isn't for you. (Same thing applies if you adored every single minute of law school.)

Yet if you were only going to do the lawyer thing until you figured out what you were really going to do with your life... you're in luck.

This is the ultimate companion for lawyers who want to escape their profession but are sceptical about career counsellors. It is based on years of experience helping hundreds of confused lawyers at Escape the City, a community of motivated corporate professionals who want to 'do something different' with their careers.

Easy to read, it has inspiring anecdotes, frameworks from internationally leading career change experts, and immediately actionable tips and exercises to help you build a strategy for your career transition.

TABLE OF
CONTENTS

ABOUT THE AUTHOR 1

INTRODUCTION 3

[1] GETTING UNSTUCK 13

[2] TRACING HIDDEN BARRIERS 33

[3] FINDING ALIGNMENT 57

[4] FACING RESISTANCE 81

[5] EXPERIMENTING STRATEGICALLY 97

[6] PREPARING FINANCIALLY 125

[7] EMBRACING RENEWAL 154

[8] FINAL THOUGHTS 173

A FEW MORE STORIES 182

ACKNOWLEDGEMENTS 202

REFERENCES 204

ABOUT THE AUTHOR

As an early employee of Escape the City, a community of motivated corporate professionals who want to 'do something different' with their careers, Adele Barlow found herself quasi-counselling top graduates from the world's leading universities. These bright millennials had followed all the rules, gotten "safe" and "sensible" jobs, then found themselves feeling lost. After accidentally moonlighting as their makeshift therapist and writing for the Huffington Post, Adele trained in cognitive behavioural coaching with the British Psychological Society and started boutique publishing house Outbound Books™.

Adele led the global Escape community, built the Escape School in London, and designed Escape's core education curriculum. In her final year of university, she co-founded an award-winning social enterprise that created digital campaigns for charities. Over the past decade she has also produced digital marketing content and events for various startups, corporations and agencies.

Read more about the author here: www.adelebarlow.com
Read more about the publisher here:
www.outbound-books.com
Join Escape the City here: www.escapethecity.org

INTRODUCTION

"In a chronically leaking boat, energy devoted to changing vessels is more productive than energy devoted to patching leaks."

-Warren Buffett

On a residential road in North London, Mark sat on the number 73 bus wondering what the hell he had done. Only a few hours ago, he had been an Associate at his firm. Now his days were numbered as he had just handed in his notice. His mind felt foggy as he tried to conceptualise potential futures but among the confusion one thing felt crystal clear.

"I knew for sure that I didn't want my manager's life," Mark confessed. "He was a Senior Associate and doing the same thing as I was but getting paid more... he had two young kids, lived an hour out of London and worked until 10pm every night."

Over the years, the Senior Associate had also developed Irritable Bowel Syndrome from the stress of the profession and as a result, during quiet meetings, his stomach would sound like a broken washing machine. Mark knew he did not want this bodily soundtrack in his own future.

I heard stories like this hundreds of times while working with Escape the City ("Escape"), a community of motivated corporate professionals who want to do something different with their careers. As Escape's Education Director, I produced many events over the years that brought me into contact with some of the sharpest people I've ever met.

However, no matter how book-smart they were, many of these corporate professionals were clueless when it came to steering their careers. They knew that they eventually wanted to be doing something different but they were all haunted by the same question: if not this, then what?

WHY LAWYERS CAN'T LEAVE

Specific barriers seemed to exist for lawyers in the Escape community, illustrated in their own words below. You'll notice that the same barriers crop up in all of the stories we hear about, over and over again.

"The main problem is not being sure what to do next."

The thing stopping him from quitting tomorrow is being unsure what to do next, and the drop in income. He wants to leave the law because he doesn't think he is very good at it – he doesn't particularly enjoy it and in the specialism he is in, there doesn't seem to be scope for flexible, part time or contract working.

There was no particular turning point – he just never really enjoyed law. He would be reluctant to leave without a plan and his main problem is not being sure what to do next.

*"You don't focus on the bigger picture,
just accomplishing each stage."*

She is still developing a business idea and finds that the biggest hurdle to quitting is finding the right thing to do. She wants to leave the law because it seems to suffocate her creativity and does not enable her to play to her strengths.

She knew that she wanted to leave upon qualification, but that was years ago. Up until then, she was focused on the series of steps to go through (law school, each six month seat of training contract, qualification) without time to focus on the bigger picture, just on accomplishing each stage. Only after she had qualified did she start to question whether law was actually what she wanted to do.

"The biggest obstacle is probably financial uncertainty."

She is not actively looking to leave the law at the moment, although she is open to new opportunities and inspiration. She came to an Escape event having just been made redundant from a firm where she was not happy anyway. She had only worked at one law firm. Given the time and effort that had gone into training, she wanted to try another firm before calling it a day.

She is much happier at the current firm but does not plan to stay a lawyer forever. The biggest obstacle is financial uncertainty as her husband works for a start-up and his financial position isn't set in stone right now.

"I wouldn't want to leave without a definite plan."

Her game plan is to stay where she is while she is happy and satisfied with what she is doing but to keep an eye out for other interesting opportunities, and move on if she is not happy.

If she were to leave, she would want some form of income lined up, even just to pay the bills, along with a definite plan of what she wanted to do and the steps she intended to take to get there. Sometimes she wonders how she has ended up here.

"When you've invested a lot of time and energy, it becomes hard to change direction."

Being a lawyer wasn't always his dream – he saw it more as a stepping-stone. The thing stopping him from quitting tomorrow is making sure he has a solid plan in place – a holding job, and enough savings to keep him going.

The biggest hurdles to quitting are mainly financial – mortgage payments and other obligations. There are also other personal considerations: when you've invested a lot of time and energy into something, it becomes hard to change direction.

He wants to leave law because he doesn't find it fulfilling to be working until at least 9pm every evening, more often later, with no stake in what he is doing. He knew he wanted to leave about six months after qualification, during a busy period.

He's at a point where he can't understand why he's doing what he is doing. He is planning to save some additional funds and would ideally like to move into a quasi-legal role that is well paid but more interesting.

WHY I WROTE THIS BOOK

In my final year of my arts degree at university, I won seed funding to pursue a startup idea with my best friend. This introduced me to the world of digital media and startups. Two years later, I grew tired of the emotional roller coaster and financial insecurity of the entrepreneurial life, so I decided to start looking into getting a 'real' job by going to law school.

I dropped out of law school after three weeks because it was impossible to ignore the evidence that I would be a terrible lawyer. As early on as my first Torts class, it became crystal-clear that I was feigning interest in everything that was being taught. I was only 22 at the time but I was old enough to know that it is impossible to excel at something that bores you as much as Torts bored me.

The process of constructing my exit strategy included feeling like a total moron and being paralysed by a generous buffet of fears (ranging from "How do I tell Dad?" to "What the hell am I going to do now?").

To self-medicate, I bathed in the words of self-help authors ("change is the only constant" came up a lot) and I found ways to touch potential alternative realities. During law school, I was also doing an internship at a digital media investment firm. On the days when I didn't have class, I got to know older adults who had built interesting, rewarding careers in digital media. This helped me to put my own twenty-something navel-gazing into perspective.

My transition was different to the one that you might be considering now. A 22-year-old's brief stint at law school is hardly comparable to someone at a later stage of life with an established legal career. Still, my experience indicates that I understand the appeal of the security and prestige tied to a legal career. Perhaps because I almost became a lawyer myself, the plight of lawyers within the Escape community has always resonated with me especially deeply.

While my transition might have been much easier – as I was not leaving behind a steady salary and track record – it still came with meaningful lessons that I often refer to when speaking to Escape members, such as the idea that we sometimes run away from that which we most desire. Looking back, I always wanted an entrepreneurial career, but law school was an incredibly convenient way to distract myself from dreams that both thrilled and terrified me.

I eventually discovered that fear can be a green light to keep going down a new path, instead of being a stop sign. If something scares us in a way that makes us feel alive and excited, it usually strikes a chord in us because what is at stake is meaningful.

WHAT YOU CAN EXPECT

When I was making the decision about whether or not to leave law school, there were a number of resources that deeply influenced me, which I found myself recommending to Escape members over the years. My goal with this book was to condense those resources into an easy-to-read companion that could function as a reference for anyone considering leaving the law.

Instead of having to schedule various meetings with lawyers who have gone on to do other things with their careers, I've taken their experiences and condensed their wisdom here, so that you can move forwards faster with your own decision-making process.

If you've ever questioned how others transitioned away from the legal profession, you'll get specific insights into how and why they did so. If you've ever wondered what those ex-lawyers wish that they had been told before they made the leap, you'll see the key messages that keep emerging.

When we're done, you'll be able to understand whether or not it's time to move away from the law, and how you can structure your escape intelligently.

WHAT WE SHALL COVER

After leaving Escape the City, I trained in cognitive behavioural coaching with the British Psychological Society. After years of working with hundreds of young professionals through Escape, I wanted to summarise my observations and so I came up with the LEARNER™ framework that I often apply whenever someone talks about feeling 'stuck' in their career. We will use the LEARNER framework throughout this book:

L = LESSON (How is this an opportunity?)

The first chapter looks at the meaning of an impasse, which is often mistaken for a quarter-life crisis. There are six phases of impasse, yet you can only progress through each of them when you accept and increase your self-awareness instead of resisting or running away from what is going on inside you. An impasse can involve negative or painful feelings but it is actually an opportunity to grow further into the person we have always wanted to become. There is a valuable lesson to be gained from any impasse.

E = EXCAVATION (Where is it coming from?)

We will then trace the hidden barriers that stop a person from switching careers. There are always going to be mental barriers when it comes to any kind of transition. Prescribing actions is not enough. Behavioural change starts with becoming more aware of how your mind sometimes hold you back from what you actually want. As explore this excavation process, we will look at the theories of Martin Seligman, often described as the father of the positive psychology movement.

A = ALIGNMENT (Which values win?)

When finding your way out of impasse, you need to use your mind, heart, and gut instinct to make decisions, and this is what we cover in the third chapter. A coach can help you to reconnect with your dormant decision-making instincts, which are often devalued in high-pressure environments like law where the rational mind is encouraged beyond all else. Whenever you are lost, it is your values that will lead you back home. We explore the alignment of your values with your career.

R = RESISTANCE (What are the obstacles?)

We investigate how self-sabotage and resistance can come in a number of forms. Some common traps include "all or nothing" thinking, looking externally first and turning your career change into a never-ending project as opposed to a reality. We look at the Kurt Lewin model of change, commonly referred to as Unfreeze, Change, Freeze (or Refreeze). It is normal to feel incredibly unstable during the 'change' phase, before we have experienced the 'refreezing' stage.

N = NOVELTY (Which experiments will help?)

Next, we explore how building a career in the 21st century is different from the process that previous generations experienced. An impasse means that the existing arrangement needs to change and introducing novelty through strategic experimentation helps to structure that update. Learning, experimenting, and networking are the best ways of opening yourself up to new options. Changing careers happens when you craft experiments, shift connections, and reframe past events into a new story.

E = ENTERPRISE (Is this financially viable?)

We tackle the financial aspect of transition in Chapter 6. There are certainly ways to earn a living from your legal skills that do not necessarily require you to remain in your current role if the hours or demands are too overwhelming. We look at the financial questions that come with career change and how to treat your career as an enterprise.

R = REVIEW (Which metrics matter?)

Lastly, we explore how a grieving process alongside career change is perfectly normal. We look at how to review your career change and how to focus on the metrics that matter.

WHAT WE SHALL AVOID

I will not be telling you what you should do with your life. Only you can find the answers that you are looking for. My hope is that this book catalyses your own decision-making process through introducing you to a variety of perspectives and stories.

Leaving any job is risky. But there are ways to mitigate the risk and this book is a tool to doing just that. It is designed to help you begin thinking about alternative careers but it is just a beginning.

No book written by someone you have never met is going to be able to tell you what to do. So do take this book for what it is: a step toward a more fulfilling career. While I can't give you the answers, I can hopefully help you to find your own answers within yourself.

[1]

GETTING UNSTUCK

"Talk to a surprising number of people who went to law school, and you'll hear a remarkably similar story: There is a moment, usually in your second year (and often, precisely when you're in the middle of an interview, convincing the interviewer – and yourself – just how passionate you are about the intricacies of contract law), that a creeping feeling begins to take hold. All of a sudden, you realize that this pricey, hard, and tedious thing you got yourself into is not at all what you want to do for the rest of your life."

Devo Ritter

I asked my friend how she was and she gave a pretty honest reply.

"I feel like crap, I look like crap – don't deny it and try to be nice, I haven't slept properly all week – and I've just stopped caring about what I'm doing," she sighed. "They're not paying me enough for what they expect from me."

Well, you're in the right place, I thought. This room was full of people who, I guessed by their very presence, felt the same pain as her.

It was a Tuesday evening in London's Piccadilly Circus and about 60 lawyers were trickling into a conference room in the Hub Westminster co-working space for an Escape event about leaving the law.

My friend and I stood to one side. She reminded me why we had chosen to run this very event.

"I could not be more ready for tonight," she declared. "Give it to me. Seriously. I need to get out."

Over the last few months, we'd spent hours talking about what she'd been feeling, which, I'd realised since working with Escape the City, was more common than she thought. In fact, it almost seemed strange if over-worked lawyers *hadn't* felt what she had been feeling.

As she had explained, it wasn't depression, but it felt like being in some kind of perpetual hangover... without alcohol involved. When alcohol did get involved, it only seemed to make things worse.

The question lingering in her 3am thoughts: "What is it that I *really* want to do with my life? Why the hell can't I decide? What is wrong with me for not knowing?"

Rationally she knew that she was lucky to have her job but emotionally she felt like it was preventing her from doing whatever it was that she was actually meant to be doing.

As she smoothed her black pencil skirt and mustered up a smile, I thought about a book that I'd recommended to people in her position countless times, although I had never before mentioned it to her.

I knew that she barely had time to do anything outside of work, let alone read for pleasure – but the book wasn't just some corny self-help tome or clichéd careers guide.

The book – *Getting Unstuck: A Guide to Discovering Your Next Career Path* – was written by business psychologist and researcher Timothy Butler, the director of career development programs at Harvard Business School.

Maybe it had been the link to Harvard that gave me the impetus to trust the book more than I trusted most career guides, but as soon as I had started reading it, I had been hooked.

The main message I got from the book was that breakdowns can lead to breakthroughs. Sometimes when things seem to be falling apart, they can actually be falling into place, if we surrender to the negative emotions that usually we try so hard to resist.

THE EMERGENCE OF IMPASSE

It is all too easy to float through the motions of life on autopilot. As we start to take responsibility for our own lives, a lot of millennials fall into what mainstream culture labels 'the quarterlife crisis' – a term that I have grown to violently dislike, as I think it oversimplifies what Butler more accurately labels 'an impasse.'

An impasse, as Butler describes, is when "we try to push our way forward using our old views and methods. Soon we realise this is not working and find ourselves at a dead end. Energy and inspiration begin to evaporate; our conviction seems less certain."

"We begin to hear the stinging voice of our inner critic and old doubts about our ability and our direction return. We seem to be both sinking and moving backward," he says, summing up exactly what I had seen countless Escape members experiencing.

Butler goes on to explain the point that illustrates the crux of his entire book: "These feelings at first may bring alarm, but we must come to recognise them as signals that an important process is beginning. Being at impasse is a developmental necessity."

We're conditioned to run away when things are hard. However, Butler talks about stepping into any psychological pain and seeing it as an important signal that how we make sense of the world is about to change.

SELF-ATTRIBUTION

Butler explains that for most people, an impasse sneaks up unexpectedly and at first presents itself through feelings of frustration, a significant down mood and what may feel like the first flickering signs of depression.

What can block us from fully moving through the impasse is the guilt that comes with self-attribution, as in, the suspicion that there is something wrong with *us* for even feeling this way. This involves thoughts like, "I'm not proceeding correctly, I'm failing, I'm not living up to my potential, I'm not doing my job the way that it should be done, I can't see ahead and I can't get motivated."

This is a feeling shared across the globe. As a former corporate lawyer and current Escape member from New Zealand shared:

"I felt guilty for complaining about a job that, on paper, is a very good job, well respected and offers a good salary. I questioned why I was so unhappy when many others before me (including my Dad) had just 'sucked it up' and embraced it as a good solid career without searching for the 'dream job'. A lot of my friends

relate to this, thinking that we are being needy or demanding by questioning what we are doing and wanting to move away from the law. This is just another way we blame ourselves for being at this point."

Guilt is not a productive emotion. The more productive way through impasse is to focus on self-acceptance as well as acknowledging that you are the only person who can experience, understand, and navigate yourself out of what you are going through.

THE PROTEAN CAREER

Before you can begin mapping an escape route, it's important to notice how careers in the twenty-first century have changed. Part of the underlying friction that I see Escape members struggling with comes from the fact that many millennials seem to be searching for simple answers in an era where careers have become increasingly complex.

If we look at the history of career construction, we can begin to understand the current landscape. Up until the 1800s, jobs were not specific positions with specifically defined boundaries but were actually a set of constantly changing tasks.

Craftsmen and itinerant workers searched for work where it was available and updated their skills as necessary – they took responsibility for their own employability. Contracts tended to last for the duration of a particular project or piece of work and were short-term in nature.

Employment models changed after the industrial revolution, when growth in the manufacturing and finance sectors gave birth to the organisational career. These organisations defined roles and structured jobs more tightly than before, meaning that employees began to expect a job for life as contracts became longer-term.

Employers essentially managed careers, which tended to be linear, hierarchical, and relatively secure, particularly in larger organisations.

As the twentieth century came to a close, organisations underwent widespread, ongoing downsizing, and restructuring in response to ever-increasing competitive pressures. This changed career and employment patterns significantly and organisations could no longer guarantee job security, meaning that the relationship between individual and organisation became more short-term and transactional in its nature.

This means that the traditional organisation career, which was once perceived as the norm, is now seen by many career researchers as more relevant to the last century. In the future, we are likely to see careers characterised by flexible employment contracts, multiple employers, lateral job moves and multiple career changes – also known as the protean career, as described by career academic Stuart Hall:

"The protean career is a process which the person, not the organization, is managing [their career]... the criterion of success is internal (psychological success), not external."

This model emphasises taking responsibility for your own career instead of relying on an employer to draft and map your career for you. It emphasises employability through embracing a lattice-like career of inter-organisational moves and life-long learning – as opposed to climbing a career ladder. The protean career is driven by personal career choices and a search for self-fulfillment.

I often saw when talking to Escape members that half the battle of mapping a new career was accepting that it would follow a different type of blueprint to the one that their parents might have been used to.

George Bernard Shaw said, "Life isn't about finding yourself, life is about creating yourself." Never before has that creation been so complex. The choices that millennials are faced with are far more varied than the ones our parents dealt with.

There are new stresses involved in constructing the self. We live in an age where our career becomes a key playground through which to derive a sense of identity, fulfillment, and meaning. A job is no longer just a way to pay the bills.

With new freedoms come new anxieties. There is a new existential stress among millennials that comes with having that very ability to choose their own path. In many ways, we are liberated without necessarily being empowered: more doors are now open, but we are not always adequately informed about what lies beyond them or what it takes to pass through.

VUCA has become a trendy managerial acronym used to describe or reflect on the volatility, uncertainty, complexity and ambiguity of general conditions and situations. When applied to the subject of millennial career choices, it explains the proliferation of the 'quarter life crisis' and the new stress that I notice among ambitious peers.

When you believe that you have the power to create whichever 'self' you desire to construct, the privilege of being able to participate in that construction is a double-edged sword. To believe that you can become whoever you want to be is an incredible gift. However, if you *can* become whoever you want to be, and you *fail* to then you become the one to blame. You are the faulty architect. So in this new era of heightened confidence also comes the potential for a harder fall.

In previous generations, identity was largely inherited where these days it is now constructed. Today we are all architects of our own identities, yet we are still learning how to put together career blueprints. This is why the impasse has become increasingly prevalent.

THE PHASES OF IMPASSE

As Butler describes, "A life impasse fulfills a specific purpose in our psychological development. It is a call to return to and integrate aspects of our emotional and psychological being that have been set aside because of competing life circumstances." In that sense, any impasse is an important learning opportunity and can help us to learn new ways of interacting with the world.

Butler explains that there are six phases of impasse, as described below. These phases are not rigidly linear – there is constant back and forth between the different stages.

1. SENSING
The first phase is to sense an impasse. The automatic response, and the one which everyone takes, is to keep on going anyway and pushing through – pulling more hours, trying to shuffle around the current arrangement, trying to figure out how to make the current situation work through adjusting small daily habits.

2. GETTING STUCK

The second phase sees the crisis deepening – the small adjustments don't seem to be working and emotionally there is a sense of being stuck. Old issues emerge and the inner critic flares up and becomes louder than ever.

3. REALISING

The third phase is to realise that the entire old way of thinking isn't working. We begin to accept the situation with a more open outlook.

4. OPENING UP

The fourth phase pushes us to listen to what we may not have heard before and to open up to new information. We are pushed to new levels of understanding and we are forced to go deeper with exploring why we are stuck.

5. BECOMING AWARE

The fifth phase is an increased self-awareness of what environments we enjoy, our deepest values, what matters to us. As we grow older we have the possibility of gaining insight into our own patterns and our own deepest interests and whether or not they are expressed through certain roles.

6. ACTING

The sixth and final phase is about taking action, without which the benefits of an impasse cannot really be experienced. We take some action that shows that we have been through the impasse, learned what we needed to observe, and can now go out into the world armed with these lessons.

SAM'S STORY:
"THE ACCIDENTAL LAWYER"

Sam worked with us at Escape after leaving a legal career, to learn more about content and marketing. As I learned more about his transition, I began to appreciate the eloquence with which he expressed his story. We will follow Sam's story throughout this book.

His episode exemplifies what Butler describes and the first stage of Sam's story demonstrates what the initial stages of impasse often look like.

* * *

I was a solicitor for a while, though I never really felt like one. I had no affinity with the profession, the role or the work, and as far as I could tell, I was really only a solicitor according to my CV and my LinkedIn profile.

Calling myself a solicitor was kind of like calling yourself a guitarist because you happen to have a guitar in your bedroom: the accoutrements don't necessarily reflect the substance.

Such was my almost immediate disillusionment with my corporate role that I spent the huge majority of my time thinking about what I would do when I left law. My next move was the kind of thing I was passionate about and could get excited about. I couldn't get excited about law.

I had fallen haphazardly into a legal training contract – a result of it being an easy option, the obvious choice following my law degree and a relative financial boon. Doubtless my decision was also in part down to cowardice, and embarrassingly, a preoccupation with maintaining the perception of parity with my peer group. This is the single most ridiculous reason for my choice, but it seems to be a common pressure in terms of career decisions.

I knew after a week that I was in the wrong career, and although I regularly challenged myself to re-commit, re-motivate and reassess how I could get the most from my job, it was useless: I was in the wrong place doing the wrong thing.

I tried working with different people and I tried doing different work. I tried pretending that I cared about the projects I was working on, and I tried a slapdash approach based on a public display of not caring. None of this made the experience any less of a chore. To spend such a huge amount of time persevering with an endless chore dressed up as a corporate treadmill is soul-destroying. I didn't want to be there, and I had no enthusiasm for the work that I was supposed to be doing.

Well, no matter, I thought; decision made, now get on with your life. Just bag a couple of international secondments and get out of there. And that's what I did: I spent six months criss-crossing beaches in Southeast Asia, followed by six months in a Jacuzzi in Moscow. Not a bad stint, certainly. But the fact that I had two such incredible experiences and still maintained such an overriding negative impression demonstrates the extent to which I felt stifled by my job.

For all the beaches and banyas that my sojourns abroad had offered me, I had spent two and a half years doing unstimulating, unfulfilling and seemingly inconsequential work. I had sacrificed an awful lot in terms of evenings, weekends and relationships – essentially my freedom to enjoy life.

Ultimately, I had sacrificed my happiness, and the question I kept asking myself was why?

There are a number of easy answers: stability, security later in life, a means to an end ("put in your time now so as to set yourself up for later on"), and probably the most persistent justification of all – money.

The money was good, of course (although some way from being as good as my peers working in finance). And I happily spent the money (inevitably, you spend what you earn), although I did so frivolously, seeking short-term gratification in order to make up for the drudgery of my normal working life.

Sadly, short-term gratification is inherently illusory. What's worse is that I found that even this was undermined by a nagging preoccupation with my professional dissatisfaction. It wasn't that I couldn't switch off from the work (I can't claim to have been switched on that much!) but rather that I couldn't switch off from a sense of neither fulfilling my potential, nor committing to my aspirations.

I couldn't reconcile the work that I was doing with the notion that I hadn't spent years of effort jumping through academic hoops to end up with such a dismal sense of apathy regarding my work. It was all so dispiriting.

Ultimately, my problem was show-stoppingly simple and abundantly clear to me: my work negated my happiness. And to buy into work that has that kind of impact takes some justification.

* * *

While different things can trigger each person's impasse, what each trigger has in common is that it is a wake-up call. As Butler says, an impasse is "a request for us to change our way of thinking about ourselves and our place in the world."

Here are some examples of what triggered others to start considering a career change.

JIM
Co-founder of Blunt Communications, a PR consultancy, and BragItUp.com, which curates the web's best deals.

"My wife had recently given birth to our son George when I had an appraisal meeting with a number of partners. There were no problems with the appraisal until one of the partners suggested that I should be writing more legal articles.

At that point I thought that they didn't really know much about me and that the last thing I would want to do, with a young child at home, would be to write an esoteric piece that nobody would read. I had also reached a point where I was working on other businesses, and thought, 'that should be me instructing lawyers!'"

DEANNE
A creative script editor and producer in television and film, with a wide range of skills in all areas of production.

"I had a niggling sense that there was more to life than reading corporate finance documents until 2am. There was also a desire to try and make a go of the only career path that had ever interested me, even if I failed.

Having to go into work on a Saturday with a raging hangover and a bucket of KFC to spend 12 hours reviewing documents that bored me silly was a definite low point. But it was more a growing sense of doom that I had made a terrible mistake with my choice of career and if I didn't do something soon, I could be trapped there forever."

ALISON
Operates Chez Serre Chevalier, a boutique UK tour operator offering tailor-made holidays.

"Like most solicitors, by four of five years after qualifying you start thinking about the future and, in particular, whether it may be possible to become a partner.

I started thinking about the bigger picture: did I want to live in London for the foreseeable future; was I prepared to continue with the working demands of a city lawyer; and were there other things I would like to achieve?

As I was pondering these issues, my partner's cousin Jackie, who had been diagnosed with terminal cancer and was just two years older than me, very sadly passed away. It was a huge shock to us both. It made us realise that it is all too easy to talk about changing your life, but if we were serious about following our dreams then it was time to take a risk and do something about it."

THE PATH THROUGH IMPASSE

If you're reading this, it is more than likely that you're at the first, second or third stage of an impasse. However, to move through the impasse, it must first be accepted. Instead of avoiding and fearing it, each of these Escape members built the ability to accept and experience darker times as part of a longer cycle of creativity and change. As Butler explains, "They are able to say, 'This condition, this feeling state is *something I am going through,* rather than *something I am.*"

Butler's book helps you move through your own impasse by outlining the actions you can take. Action helps you to gather new experiences and new data points for your decision-making process. The alternative is failing to take action and remaining stuck in the same cycle of frustration and despair without any information about new routes or possibilities.

How we move through impasse is explored in the following chapters. We explore how to trace the hidden barriers preventing you from starting to escape, how to assess where you're at and how to map an escape route through experimenting strategically and preparing financially.

An impasse is like your computer's operating system prompting you to update the software. It is a signal that our cognitive map of life and the way we fit into the world is outdated. We all carry ideas about our place in the world yet that cognitive map never completely matches reality, which is forever changing. When our typical approaches fail, it is a sign that we need to alter our entire outlook and treatment of the problem.

That is why, at the event that night in the Hub Westminster, I felt mixed emotions as I told my friend to take her seat. Of course it's not fun to sense melancholy in someone you care about. But part of me was excited for her. I knew that she wasn't having a 'quarter-life crisis' – she was at the first stage of an impasse. And I was curious to see where it would take her.

IN A NUTSHELL

» The career choices that our generation faces are more complex than those of our predecessors and so we are likely to face an impasse more frequently than our parents did.

» An impasse is a completely natural psychological stage: it often looks like a down mood, frustration, or depression, but without going through this growth process, we cannot grow, change, and – eventually – live more fully in a larger world. Any impasse is an opportunity to learn a new way of interacting with the world.

» There are six phases of impasse, yet we can only progress through each of them when we accept and increase our self-awareness instead of resisting or running away from what is going on inside us.

FURTHER RESOURCES

» Butler, Timothy. Getting Unstuck: A Guide to Discovering Your Next Career Path. Harvard Business Review, 2009. Print.

» Hall, Sam. "Is It Worth Being Unhappy in Your Profession?" Escape the City. 26 Mar. 2014. Web. 10 Nov. 2014. <http://www.escapethecity.org/blog/get-unstuck/worth-unhappy-profession>

» Ritter, Devo. "What to Do When You Don't Want to Be a Lawyer Anymore." The Muse. 21 Mar. 2014. Web. 9 June 2015. <https://www.themuse.com/advice/life-after-law-what-to-do-when-you-dont-want-to-be-a-lawyer-anymore>

» Clarke, Marilyn. "Plodders, Pragmatists, Visionaries and Opportunists: Career Patterns and Employability." Career Development International, 14.1 (2009): 8-28.

» Clarke, Marilyn. "Understanding And Managing Employability In Changing Career Contexts." Journal of European Industrial Training, 32.4 (2008): 258-284.

» Hall, D T. "Protean Career, Definition(s) of." *Work and Family Researchers Network.* 18 Sept. 2011. Web. 1 Dec. 2014. <https://workfamily.sas.upenn.edu/glossary/p/protean-career-definitions>

EXERCISES

» Read more about Timothy Butler's approach to impasse in this article:

Lagace, Martha. "Feeling Stuck? Getting Past Impasse." *Harvard Business School Working Knowledge.* 25 Apr. 2007. Web. 10 Nov. 2014. <http://hbswk.hbs.edu/item/5548.html/>

» Do Timothy Butler's 100 Jobs exercise. As he describes: "It has nothing to do with jobs. It's a way of helping a person identify the core themes, dynamic tensions, and images that are trying to emerge at this particular moment in his or her life."

» You can find a version of the 100 Jobs exercise, adapted from *Getting Unstuck,* here: http://alumni-prod-acquia.gsb.stanford.edu//sites/default/files/The_100_Jobs_Exercise.pdf (Chan, Andy. *The 100 Jobs Exercise.* 2008)

HOW I ESCAPED: BELLA'S STORY

"Once I had got comfortable with the idea that I wasn't throwing in the towel and giving up, but rather making a conscious decision to better myself and my career then any hesitation about leaving the law faded."

I left because I had become disillusioned with the law. Lawyers are, in general, very intelligent, driven, motivated people so when you spend years managing document reviews, for example, you start to question what you are doing. You start to question whether there is anything else you could be doing where your skills can be used in a way that is more fulfilling, not only for yourself but where you can actually make a more significant contribution to the lives of others.

Now, I've taken up an executive director position at a not-for-profit organisation in Australia. Founded on the concept that a healthy environment, a healthy community and a healthy lifestyle are inextricably linked, the organisation runs and supports a variety of programs that aspire to enrich people's lives and enable people to improve their mental and physical health through real interactions with nature.

The turning point was when I moved to Belgium to work for a magic circle firm. I initially saw this as my 'wow, I've made it' moment, but soon realised that once my life was stripped back to just being all about work, a legal career was no longer what I wanted. My physical and mental health were suffering the two years I spent overseas, both in Belgium and London, and I knew that for that reason alone it was time to rethink my career.

I was fortunate to be approached by an old mentor about taking up my new role. Thankfully, my new role pays a comparable salary to my legal role, so I was able to make the transition with financial ease.

While I perhaps wouldn't have been an immediate first choice for my new employer, they were interested in my legal background as it was taken as a given that I had excellent communication, reasoning and writing skills. The organisation was in a transition phase where it was looking to take a more professional approach so my background was seen as a real positive. They acknowledged that some specific training may be needed around corporate governance and director duties to get me up to speed, and were very open about providing that for me.

When you spend so long at university and training to be a lawyer I think it is only natural that we want to see all that hard work and time pay off. I knew that life was short, but I kept telling myself that my legal career would get better.

After reading "The Escape Manifesto" by Escape the City, my mentality changed. I looked around at those colleagues above me and thought, 'do I really want to end up like them?' The work and long hours just got worse the higher you progressed and I just thought that there had to be more to life than this. Once I paused long enough to acknowledge that then the thought of leaving changed from being daunting to being really exciting.

I like to finish things that I start and to work towards and achieve the goals I set myself. Initially, leaving the law wasn't part of those goals. However, once I had got comfortable with the idea that I wasn't throwing in the towel and giving up but rather making a conscious decision to better myself and my career, then any hesitation about leaving the law faded.

I've wanted to be a lawyer since I was 15 (I'm now 32). When you spend your whole adult life working towards one goal, and that goal takes up all your time, you find that other passions and interests either don't exist or get pushed aside. The lack of other passions was one of the most confronting things I had to acknowledge once I realised that I wanted to leave the law.

My only regrets are that I didn't leave the law earlier.

There was only one month between me resigning and me starting my new role, so I gave 3 weeks' notice and then relocated back to Australia.

Don't let the potential judgment you may receive from others be a reason for not leaving. It's your life! To be fair, you are not the only one thinking of making the move and you will be surprised by the support you receive.

* * *

[2]

TRACING HIDDEN BARRIERS

"How strange that the nature of life is change, yet the nature of human beings is to resist change. And how ironic that the difficult times we fear might ruin us are the very ones that can break us open and help us blossom into who we were meant to be."

-Elizabeth Lesser

About a year after that event at the Hub Westminster, one of the members who had attended appeared at the entrance of Adam Street Club, where we were running an Escape event. I recognised him as his six-foot frame stepped through the doorway although I didn't know him that well.

I remembered that his name was Scott, that he was a lawyer, and that he was a fellow Kiwi. Sure enough, he addressed me as "mate" and then asked, "How's it going?"

I told Scott a little bit about what I'd been working on at Escape. As he was wearing a suit, I assumed that he was still in his old job. I was curious as to what might have changed since I'd last seen him and something in my face must have asked the question before I voiced it.

He grinned at me, and before I could ask what *he* had been up to, he blurted out, "I quit!"

Regardless of what I blurted back (most likely something along the lines of "Wow" or "How?"), he steamrolled along with his story, talking about how he handed in his resignation, then went back home to New Zealand for a couple of weddings, and now, he explained, "I'm back here, in a new job. *Not* as a lawyer."

Scott smiled proudly. In his voice, I heard the same pride of a new father showing off a wallet photo of his smiling baby. Except in this case, he had created a new career, which I guess warranted just as much of a celebration.

I wasn't sure what was physically appropriate, as it seemed too strange to hug him, even though I really wanted to. Instead I did some weird shoulder-punch gesture and congratulated him.

SCOTT'S STORY: "USE FEAR TO GALVANISE YOU"

I had reached a point in my legal career where I was acutely aware that in order to progress I would have to fully commit both to law as a career and to my firm (or find a role elsewhere). It therefore seemed like an opportune time to ask myself some hard questions: "Am I passionate about law as a career? Is this what I want to do for the rest of my working life? If I walk away from law what else is out there and will I have any transferrable skills?"

The answer to the first and second questions was "No". As soon as I knew that it was clear to me that I had to go.

Everyone has difficult times in their legal career (or any career), but in the six months prior to making the decision I increasingly felt that, despite spending the significant majority of my waking hours behind a desk poring through thousands of documents, painstakingly piecing together the background to complex disputes and drafting lengthy witness statements to support the client's position, the work I was doing wasn't appreciated.

Rather, it was simply expected and demanded. I know law is a service industry and the remuneration is generally considered to be very good (unless you break it down into an hourly wage), but there is nothing worse than being grilled by a client for something trivial after having worked all weekend to meet their deadline. That, combined with the sense of dread I felt creeping in every Sunday about the impending work week, helped me realise that I had to make some radical changes.

Having realised it was time to go, the next question was, when? As it happened, I had a family event in New Zealand that I wanted to make the effort to attend (despite being on the other side of the world). I had no annual leave left, so in order to make this happen, I had to quit. This actually made things easier, as it felt like there was no alternative. I knew that money would become an issue very quickly, so I started saving as much as I could to finance the transition. The risk of running out of money would cloud any decision-making process so it was important to remove that from the decision.

My biggest concern about leaving was whether I would find work outside of the law. Were my skills transferrable and, if not, would I have to start again? I spent the next two months talking to people within the business community, my peers in the legal industry and pretty much anyone who would listen about what lay beyond the law. I read a lot of the material online at escapethecity.org and went to a number of their seminars, including one on "Leaving the Law".

The seminar was excellent as it made me realise that I wasn't crazy and that there are a lot of other lawyers out there who have reached the same or similar conclusions about their careers. It became clear to me from my discussions that many of the skills I had learnt in the law could be utilised in a career in project management. In order to test this I sat my Project Management qualification (PRINCE2) over the course of two weekends. My results were good so I handed in my resignation.

I didn't attempt to get a job before I quit because I couldn't focus on anything other than law. I knew there was a considerable risk that I would be out of work for some time but I decided that this risk could be harnessed, as it would galvanise me into action rather than act as a noose around my neck.

The general attitude of friends and family to my resignation and decision to leave law was very supportive once I explained my reasons. Many of my lawyer friends are heading down the same path so they were naturally very supportive and curious to see how I fared outside the law.

After I quit I did some consultancy work for my old law firm on an interesting case for three weeks then I returned to New Zealand for a month. During this time I interviewed for a potential project management role which had come up through a personal contact that was aware that I had just stepped away from the law. I was very fortunate to land that role and I've been working as an interim Project Manager in a logistics company for the past nine months.

My role gives me direct contact with a large number of business units and employees within the company. I work directly for the CFO and CEO and this has given me invaluable insight into the management and daily running of a large multinational company.

My background as a lawyer has proven very useful so far. The discipline, critical thinking, analysis, stakeholder management and time management skills have stood me in good stead. All of these are essential for effective project management.

Looking back, the hardest thing was handing in my resignation. It felt at the time that I was going to step off a cliff into a career free-fall. I realise now that this was irrational (though entirely understandable). There will never be a right time to quit or make a change. In terms of advice for anyone contemplating leaving the law, I would say that as soon as you know that you want out, start planning and set yourself a hard stop date to resign.

If it helps, put a physical event in place immediately after the resignation date so you are working towards something. Don't worry if you haven't figured out what you are going to do or if you haven't landed that next role before you resign. After you get the weight of resignation off your shoulders you will find it is much easier to make decisions about the future.

Back yourself. Do your research, make a plan and then push the button. Use the fear to galvanise you into action.

* * *

PSYCHOLOGICAL EXCAVATION

On the way home after seeing him at the event, I had my earphones on and 'Home' by Phillip Phillips trickled onto my Spotify: "Settle down, it'll all be clear…"

I thought about all the other lawyers who had come to that Hub Westminster event, some of whom I'd kept in touch with. Half of them had left or were in the process of leaving or making plans to leave; half seemed to be remaining right where they were.

As my close friend who had 'felt like crap' had pointed out, while it had been nice to hear various stories from lawyers who had left, she had found it hard to connect how their stories could be applied to her own situation.

I thought about the other Escape members I knew who had been at the same event but had left with a completely different outlook. They had already made up their minds to leave and the event had only confirmed to them that they were on the right path.

Others were maybe never going to leave law and the event had just been a reminder that somewhere out there was other people living fulfilling careers.

The song kept playing: "Don't pay no mind to the demons / They fill you with fear / The trouble it might drag you down / If you get lost, you can always be found..." I thought about how all lawyers face the barriers that were outlined in the introduction, and the limitations of what any book, event, or external force could give a person.

As we previously explored, these seem to be the main barriers facing most lawyers wanting to leave the profession:

- "You don't focus on the bigger picture, just accomplishing each stage."

- "The biggest obstacle is probably financial uncertainty."

- "I wouldn't want to leave without a definite plan."

- "When you've invested a lot of time and energy, it becomes hard to change direction."

If we look at those barriers objectively, it seems obvious that all a person would need to do to overcome those barriers would be:

- Carving out time and space to zoom out on the bigger picture;

- Decreasing financial uncertainty;

- Discovering what to do next;

- Changing direction even after investing a lot of time and energy.

Obviously these are not straightforward overnight tasks. However, Scott managed to do all of those things, as did many other Escape members. What I learned was that when it comes to transition, prescribing actions alone is not that helpful, because they do not always address the root barriers.

The core barriers to transition are often psychological. If you are unaware of how your mind can be getting in the way of your happiness, your mind can start controlling your actions, even when those actions lead you away from happiness.

Rob Archer, a career psychologist that we often partner with at Escape the City, often talks about how our mind is not our friend. We assume that our minds want what is best for us. However, as a trained lawyer, your mindset can often be primed to *prevent* happiness.

WHAT IS REALLY STOPPING YOU?

Dr Martin Seligman, Ph.D. is the Fox Leadership Professor of Psychology at the University of Pennsylvania and the former President of the American Psychological Association.

Among his 20 books, one is called Authentic Happiness: Using the New Positive Psychology to Realise Your

Potential for Lasting Fulfillment. Within that is a chapter entitled, "Why Are Lawyers So Unhappy?"

He argues that while lawyers overtake doctors as the highest-paid professionals, they are also in poor mental health, at much greater risk than the general population of depression.

In a study completed at Johns Hopkins University, lawyers came out on top for statistically significant elevations of major depressive disorder, suffering from depression at a rate of 3.6 times higher than employed persons generally. Compared to non-lawyers, they also experience much higher rates of alcoholism and illegal drug use.

Seligman concludes: "Lawyers embody the paradox of money losing its hold. They are the best-paid professionals, and yet they are disproportionately unhappy and unhealthy. And lawyers know it; many are retiring early or leaving the profession altogether."

He explains that there are two main causes for this psychological disposition among lawyers.

PESSIMISM

Firstly, lawyers tend to have a pessimistic explanatory style, meaning that the causes of negative events tend to be seen as persistent, uncontrollable and pervasive ("It's going to last forever, and it's going to undermine everything."). An optimist, on the other hand, may see negative events as local, temporary and changeable.

While pessimistic thinking is unhelpful in most areas of life, pessimists do better at law. One study referenced in Seligman's book followed students of the Virginia Law School throughout their three years of study. Contrary to the results of previous studies looking at other areas of life, the pessimistic law students on average outperformed more optimistic students on traditional measures of achievement, such as grade point averages.

Pessimism is typically seen as a positive trait among lawyers, since perceiving troubles as pervasive and permanent is part of what constitutes prudence. Prudence helps a lawyer to spot every possible problem that might arise in any transaction. This ability *helps* the practicing lawyer who, by spotting what the non-lawyer might not see, can help his clients defend against far-fetched possibilities. Even if you don't have such prudence at the start, law school will strive to ingrain it within you. Yet while this trait might make you a good lawyer, it does not always make you a happy human being.

Low Decision Latitude

Another psychological factor that demoralises lawyers, especially junior ones, is the limited choices one believes that one has (also known as low decision latitude) in high-stress situations. Seligman also writes about a study that examined the link between job conditions and depression and coronary disease. One combination stood out as harmful to health and morale: high job demands coupled with low decision latitude. Individuals with these jobs have much higher rates of coronary disease and depression.

It is inevitable that lawyers working in big firms (particularly as trainees or newly qualified lawyers) tend to have low decision latitude by virtue of the very structure of those firms. Clear hierarchies that exist from the partner level down to the trainee level mean that it can be hard for junior lawyers to take control of their own work flow and responsibilities, not to mention the hours that they are in the office.

This structure, combined with often unrealistic client demands can mean that junior lawyers have very little opportunity to shape what their stressful working lives actually look like day to day. It is also common for junior lawyers to find themselves faced with issues that need immediate resolution, yet without the control over the situation to do just that. For example, at this level of the hierarchy, junior lawyers often lack the licence to take unsupervised actions or they lack the authority with clients to be able to progress matters themselves.

The stress, doubt and uncertainty that a junior lawyer feels in this situation is only amplified by the firm's culture – where job demands are high, and where absolute perfectionism is mandatory. It is not hard to see how weeks and months and years of experiencing such low decision latitude must take its toll on a lawyer's morale.

PESSIMISM IN ACTION

We've seen how lawyers' tendency towards pessimism, combined with the demoralisation that follows low decision latitude, are two barriers which can affect the decision to move out of law and toward a more fulfilling career.

However, the real-life impact of these factors, and particularly the tendency towards pessimism, really hit home when I found myself explaining these concepts to a lawyer friend who had been going through her own career transition.

She described the multiple decision making stages she went through when deciding to leave the law and how, at every stage (i.e., deciding to resign, looking for new opportunities and progressing job applications), her tendency towards pessimistic, or risk averse thoughts, would emerge and in some way hold her back.

After years working at a big corporate law firm, where she was required to examine and highlight risks every single day, she explained that it was easy to fall into the default pattern of questioning each decision.

However, it wasn't until she voiced these doubts to her boyfriend, a committed optimist, that she realised just how damaging those niggling pessimistic voices had been. His contrasting perspective was the wake up call to, first, identify just how damaging that learned pessimism was and, second, counteract it by incorporating his more positive comebacks into her decision-making processes.

She gave me a few (highly paraphrased) examples of how this worked when she first considered resignation – when her inner pessimist would clash with his inner optimist.

PESSIMIST: My boss will be disappointed in me.

OPTIMIST: You have to do what is right for you, not your boss, and definitely not the big law firm.

PESSIMIST: I can't leave now; it is a busy time for my team.

OPTIMIST: The team and the firm will survive – it is a big place and you're replaceable.

PESSIMIST: I don't have a good explanation for why I'm leaving and I'm embarrassed about that – I really should know what I'm doing.

OPTIMIST: Fake it until you make it. When people ask what you're doing next, say you have exciting opportunities ahead and you're excited to see where they lead. Own it and don't show doubt (even if you have some).

Pessimist: I won't survive without an income and I won't get hired.

Optimist: You are in the top few percent of educated intelligent people in the world – you have a lot to offer people and you will never be begging on the street. You have lots of marketable skills.

Pessimist: Maybe I should just suck it up and keep working – it is a safe option and, really, is it that bad?

Optimist: There are so many exciting opportunities in the world – it's a crime to stay in a job where you feel unfulfilled. Just give it a try!

Pessimist: What will my friends and family say – they will be so surprised (and potentially disappointed) that I'm looking at something so different to law after working so hard towards a legal career.

Optimist: Who cares what people say and think – you live your life, not them. The ones that love you will support you no matter what you do, especially when they see how happy you are.

Pessimist: What if I don't have any other skills outside the very narrow field I worked in?

Optimist: You're a fast learner and you didn't get through a law degree and years of toiling away in a firm without being an organised and intelligent person who could slot into a new position easily.

Pessimist: I won't put myself forward for that position because I'm not sure if it is quite right.

Optimist: What is the harm in applying? There is nothing to lose and you will gain experience in writing your cover letter and preparing your CV. You might make some good connections along the way too. Applying for a job isn't the same as committing to it.

PESSIMIST: It is too embarrassing emailing that person asking for their advice on how they got to their position. In any case, I'm sure they don't have time to respond.

OPTIMIST: People love talking about their jobs and they love talking to people who are interested in their role or industry and eager to learn. You will learn a lot from putting yourself out there.

PESSIMIST: I couldn't volunteer my services because I don't have any more hours in the day.

OPTIMIST: Busy people get stuff done. If you're really interested in finding out what that job is like, you have to give it a try and prioritise that experiment.

It is important to acknowledge the influence of pessimism on a lawyer's mindset and to counteract it wherever possible during a time of transition. As we have already explored, the simple acknowledgment of these barriers is a crucial step in your escape.

CREATING SPACE FOR THE UNKNOWN

Before embarking upon any kind of change, you almost need to prime your mind to allow that change to happen. Otherwise it becomes easy to just use 'money' as an excuse ("I'd love to pursue my passions, but I can't afford to"), as short-term financial insecurity so often can be a legitimate blocker.

We do need money to live and we often can't just walk away from our jobs without some kind of long-term financial game plan.

However, creating that financial game plan is a whole exercise in itself and we have an entire chapter dedicated to that later on. For now, I wanted to emphasise the importance of creating space for the unknown and acknowledging that a lawyer's mind is primed to spot risks and to highlight what can go wrong, instead of what can go right.

In Scott's case, he reached a point where he had to resign. Yes, he had fears, because there were risks involved. But he took the necessary steps to mitigate those risks before making the leap – he saved for the transition, he spoke to peers in the industry he was looking to enter into, and he believed that with his legal experience he would be able to find a suitable new role for himself.

This demonstrates that some fears are justified and others are irrational – yes, we *should* be scared to cross the road when there are oncoming vehicles; we *should* be scared to step beyond the metal barriers of tall buildings and cliffs. Yes, we should be *scared* of losing our primary source of income, which puts a roof over our head and food on the table. But there is no need to believe that being a lawyer is the one and only method of earning an income.

Allowing yourself to even wander off the path is only going to happen when you recognise what staying on the present path is costing you.

Sam, whose story we were introduced to in the last chapter, realised what remaining a lawyer was costing him – and his story below demonstrates that when you believe you deserve a job that makes you happy, you start to open up to the possibility that you can find it.

SAM'S STORY (CONT'D): "IS IT WORTH IT?"

How often do you hear people talk about their jobs as a means to an end? As a CV-building exercise, allowing them to demonstrate the skills and experience which should validate and give credentials for a planned accession to a job that should give them the standard of life that they hope for.

But surely this only works as a short-term pursuit? How can you justify continually jumping through hoops in pursuit of some mythical final goal?

The ever-elusive corporate carrot (partnership in the case of law) is a form of modern-day class maintenance, an illusory end-goal that so few people will ever attain, even after years spent scrambling and stagnating in the hope of doing so. It is reminiscent of industrialists telling the nineteenth century working classes to be content with their lot, suck it up, and hope that God rewards them with a place in heaven. And it gives rise to a stepping stone culture, which I for one was guilty of buying into.

I made my GCSE and A Level choices on the grounds of what I thought universities would value, and what would leave open to me the opportunities that I wanted at the time – stepping stones. I persevered with a degree that inspired little academic interest because I kept hearing how useful it would be in the future – stepping stones. I went to work on criminal prosecutions for the UN, and as great as the experience was (it was great, I won't pretend that I regret this particular stone), I was doing this for the kudos of the court and to have the clout of the UN name on my CV, not because I saw my future in international criminal law – again, stepping stones.

And then what? A job at a Magic Circle law firm. Why? Because I believed the hype: "a prestigious career, a great opportunity – oh, and don't forget that it's a difficult economic time at the moment, this will set you up nicely for something else in the future" – more stepping stones. I've been stepping (and hot-stepping) on stepping stones all of my life – but all that's really got me is the dubious distinction of having used the word 'stepping' four times in one sentence (count them!). Doubtless part of my problem is that I listened to others too much, and that I was too much of a coward to sack it all off and think about what I really wanted.

Ultimately I realised that I was just stuck on the stones. I'm only getting older and I didn't want life to pass me by. Why was I cautiously still traversing these stones when I had known how to swim for years? If I got off the stones then inevitably I'd get a bit wet, but what's a bit of adversity if it meant that ultimately I'd get to where I want to be a little faster? And if I stayed on the stones, I might never make it across. Who knows when the water might rise and leave me trapped?!

In teasing out this metaphor for my lightning-bulb moment, I'm reminded of a trip I took in Zambia back before entering the corporate world. I waded across the Zambezi just a few dozen metres away from where it crested the lip of Victoria Falls, so as to get a better view of the spectacle. Holding on to the arm of a local Zambian guy with an iron grip, I asked myself what I was doing, as the river was probably too high and it was a hugely irresponsible risk to be taking. But I made it back in one piece and had a whale of a time at Devil's Pool. And most importantly, I felt alive. What's the point of living if you don't feel alive?

A huge number of my colleagues were disillusioned with their work, the firm, and everything else that went with it. A commonly heard argument in favour of sticking it out was that it would, eventually, be worth it. The general sentiment was to do your time and make your sacrifices at this stage, so as to create the life that you want for yourself in a few years' time (the actual number of years is hugely ambiguous). I understand the logic. I'm not naïve, and I'm not looking for a bed of roses. So I asked myself the question: is it worth being unhappy in my profession?

Yes. Utterly and absolutely yes. But only, only, only if you're talking short-term unhappiness for the sake of a worthwhile and attainable (this is crucial) goal. If I have to sacrifice two years (I know, this could be much longer – I just baulk at two!) working 18-hour days and at the end of it I get a job that I love and a salary that gives me the freedom to enjoy my life, then it would be irresponsibly short-termist of me to turn it down.

Sadly, with law, there was no role further down the line, or further up the ladder, that had any hope of getting me excited or enthusiastic about pursuing. There was nothing I could aspire to that would make me happy. I didn't look at my seniors and wish I had their job. I did occasionally look at some of them and wish that they would act with a bit more human decency, but never did I want to swap places with any of them.

A lack of passion for one's job does not necessarily correlate to one's honesty to accept this, and understandably so. It's difficult to admit to yourself and to other people that you're dissatisfied with your professional choices. Our natural inclination is not to really and truly criticise the substance of our professional life, as to do so would be indicative of unhappiness with our own decisions, and ultimately disillusionment with what we are doing.

So it's easier to avoid admitting or accepting and to pretend (at least outwardly) that everything is fine. This leads to us *saying things like "well, a job is a job" and "all jobs have their downsides" or, the one that I hate the most, "oh well, I can't complain" – what kind of a lack of aspiration does that show?!*

The difficulty is that for so many people (myself included) other people's perceptions of us are really important to us and we seek comfort in their approval. I always envy people who are entirely devoid of this concern.

This is why we are more likely to donate to charity when we think someone is watching. This is why we de-tag photographs on Facebook and curate our online identity with such rigour. This is why Instagram and Pinterest work – we feel validated by meeting, and ideally surpassing, others' perceptions of us.

So just as we curate our Facebook profile and tweet strategically, we also curate our professional experiences, telling people what we'd like them to think, rather than what is actually the case. And the desire to curate is evident in the stuttered, non-committal response of people who find the question about what they actually do at work difficult. Those who love their jobs and value their work always respond easily, with passion and cogency.

And that's what I'm looking for – something that I can be enthusiastic about, something that I'm proud to talk to people about, something that I believe in.

The most impressive professional that I know left a very successful career at a luxury goods company and took a drop in both seniority and salary so he could work at a start-up whose product he was passionate about. I didn't understand his reasoning at the time, but the fluency with which he talks about his work and his passion for his job tells its own story. When your work is joyful, everything else becomes so much more enjoyable.

* * *

IN A NUTSHELL

» There are always going to be mental barriers when it comes to any kind of transition. Prescribing actions isn't enough. Behavioural change starts with becoming more aware of how your mind sometimes holds you back from what you actually want. Psychological excavation helps to uncover core barriers.

» The father of the positive psychology movement, Dr Martin Seligman, talks about how the mindset of a lawyer can be fertile ground for depression because of the pessimistic explanatory style. This means that the causes of negative events tend to be seen as persistent, uncontrollable and pervasive, as well as low decision latitude (the limited choices one believes that one has).

» Allowing yourself to even wander off the path is only going to happen when you recognise what staying on the present path is costing you. When you believe you deserve a job that makes you happy, you start to open up to the possibility that you can find it.

FURTHER RESOURCES

» Seligman, Martin. *Authentic Happiness: Using the New Positive Psychology to Realize Your Potential for Lasting Fulfillment.* Simon & Schuster Australia, 2002. Print.

» Pryor, Lisa. *The Pin Striped Prison.* Picador Australia, 2008. Print.

» Worker Bee Free – A blog for workerbees who want to break free. Meagher, Michelle. *Worker Bee Free.* 24 Dec. 2013. Web. 20 Dec. 2014. <https://workerbeefree. wordpress.com/about/>

EXERCISES

» What is the biggest mental barrier that you are facing when you think about leaving the law?

» If your best friend, who was a lawyer, came to you and confessed that they really wanted to leave the law but was facing the same mental barrier you described above – what advice would you give them? How would you help them to overcome that mental barrier?

HOW I ESCAPED: AMY'S STORY

"We lawyers need reminding that most of the world doesn't work on the worst-case-scenario model that's ingrained in most of our brains most of the time!"

In 2009 I went through a very difficult relationship breakup, which I believed was partly down to the pressures I put myself under with work and my inability to make the changes I knew I wanted.

That acted as a kind of catalyst for me to start doing something about the situation. I took a long holiday to think through some things then asked to move to part time working (which, luckily for me, was agreed). This gave me time to explore other options and simply to feel like I had control of my life back to some degree.

I haven't left the law yet, but earlier this year I did leave my permanent city job in the law. I had been working in real estate law for several years, but my first degree was in languages and I have a passion for learning about other languages and cultures and how people communicate across cultural divides. This was not even remotely indulged in my job, and there were no realistic prospects of taking my career in an international direction.

I was feeling as if I was losing touch with a whole side of myself, so I took a sabbatical in 2010/11 to explore this more by going to Morocco to do voluntary work, brush up my French, and learn about the Islamic world. At that stage I came back to my job as I wasn't ready to lose the security it offered.

Last year I started a part time MA in Intercultural Communication, which I am really enjoying. This summer I finally resigned so that I could spend two months in Thailand working with an NGO in the field of legal education. I hope to use that experience as the basis of research for my MA dissertation.

At the moment I'm trying to work out whether I can get into a career that combines these interests with law (for higher earning power and so that I get more personal satisfaction from using all of my knowledge and skills), or whether leaving the law for good is really what I want. In the meantime I'm looking for fixed term/contract work in law whilst I finish my studies. This means it can financially support me and enable me to have periods of time not working to explore other things.

I have known since I was qualified for about two years (2008) that I didn't want to stay working in the real estate field forever because of the lack of international opportunities. I have also been dissatisfied with the work/life balance of my job for a similar length of time.

Although having said that, I am the kind of person who gives their all to what they are doing so it is natural for me to work hard. It's just I was working hard towards an aim (climbing the career ladder in my field) that I didn't want. However, I felt paralysed to do anything about it because of fears about the future, not really knowing what I wanted to do instead, and lack of confidence in my ability to make changes.

Leaving my last job was the result of a long process of exploration and thought that started back in 2009. I knew that I would need to find work in London this year whilst I finish studying so had spoken to as many people as I could about fixed term or temporary work and how to go about finding this.

I'd been in contact with an agency that were very positive and told me exactly what I needed to do to get on their books when I got back from my summer abroad. I'd also evidently saved to ensure that I had enough money to tide me over for a few months. And because of having been on the lookout for other opportunities for ages, I had a good idea of the different options I could pursue to earn money when I got back.

I also had to prepare my family for the fact that I was going to leave a secure job with nothing to move on to. They're still not entirely comfortable with what I'm doing, but they know how unhappy I was stuck in my city law job so they understand what I'm trying to do.

I'm lucky enough that I bought a flat some years ago and have rented it for most of that time, so my mortgage is paid from the rental income from the flat and I don't need to worry about losing that. I was also able to find a friend to take my place in the rented flat where I live whilst I was abroad to help manage the financial outlays. Now I have to manage on my savings until I find work.

I spoke to all of my friends, at length, about leaving and what I could do instead – and I continue to do so. Also I have had an extremely supportive partner, who has been through career change himself and has a naturally slightly more positive and less risk-averse approach to life, and I have found his support and encouragement invaluable.

We lawyers need reminding that most of the world doesn't work on the worst-case-scenario model that's ingrained in most of our brains most of the time! Also I spoke to my family to try and make sure that they were prepared for the implications of the change.

Other than that I have had numerous coffees, phone calls and informal chats with a range of people in a range of different occupations as part of my explorations and information gathering. People are very generous with their time generally, and it has been encouraging and reassuring to find how many people are willing to help.

Attending Escape the City events has been a part of this. Reading books has helped too – I would recommend a book called "The (Un)happy Lawyer" which is spot on in terms of the things that lawyers worry about.

You need to surround yourself with friends and people who are positive and have a different approach to life. I like to see the positive side but the negatives still creep in occasionally (read 'often')! It took years of people patiently persuading me that I was talented and intelligent enough that I could take a risk to explore what I wanted, yet still be able to earn my living in almost any field even if it didn't work out. That kind of support is invaluable, since you won't make a move until you have some kind of core of self-belief.

The best advice I've received is having the conviction gently and persistently instilled in me that I am intelligent and capable enough to take a risk, and to still be OK if it doesn't work out. So many high achievers don't have this belief and in my view, it's fundamental to being able to change career.

* * *

[3]

FINDING
ALIGNMENT

"For the past 33 years, I have looked in the mirror every morning and asked myself: 'If today were the last day of my life, would I want to do what I am about to do today?' And whenever the answer has been 'No' for too many days in a row, I know I need to change something."

-Steve Jobs

Once upon a time, I thought that if you didn't have a straightforward answer for 'what you wanted to be when you grew up' it meant that you didn't know yourself. After talking to hundreds of Escape members over the years, I began to realise the limitations of what we can predict.

Essentially, you are what you chase. You cannot know where you will end up. But if you believe in what you are chasing, the process matters more than the illusory destination anyway. I dropped out of law school largely because of my Dad, who is truly passionate about his work.

Growing up around a father who can blissfully monologue about some obscure aspect of commercial litigation showed me what a true love for the law looks like.

Dad helped me to develop a radar for spotting the difference between someone with a genuine interest in the law and someone who is faking it. I couldn't stay in law school because my own bullshit detector was ringing too loudly for me to ignore.

As I meet more Escape members who have been qualified for years, I can see now what I suspected back then is true. It's easy to wander into law. It's difficult to get through the qualifications and the training. Yet the more a person emotionally invests in something, the harder it becomes to walk away from it.

So by the time most lawyers have put in the years and sweat and late nights and sacrifices to reach mid-level salaries, they're not just walking away from a job. They're walking away from peers, a status, and an identity, not to mention a world that they've deliberately joined and constructed for themselves.

Law is an especially difficult profession to get 'stuck' in as the barriers to entry are so high and the training you go through to become a good lawyer often ends up leaving you more aware of risk than you were before, as we explored in the previous chapter.

That's why, when it comes to escaping the law, we have to use more than just our minds. We have to tap into other parts of our decision-making abilities.

FOUR DOMAINS OF DECISION-MAKING

In *Getting Unstuck*, Timothy Butler talks about Carl Jung's four domains of consciousness: thinking, feeling, intuiting and sensing.

"In Jung's model, each of us is dominant in one of the four, and we "lead" with that domain when we attempt to understand the world and make decisions," Butler explains. "When faced with an impasse, however, no single mode of awareness can capture the impact of a significant life change."

In other words, when we are finding our way out of impasse, Butler argues that any decision must be made holistically: "from the head, the heart, and the gut." This theme of tuning into gut feelings cropped up during nearly every conversation I had with lawyers who transitioned away from the law.

As Butler explains, impasse forces us to use more of our awareness in other domains to pick the option that *feels* right: "Impasse forces us out of the comfort of our dominant mode."

This is particularly relevant for lawyers as compared to other industries; the legal sector seems to host a sub-zero tolerance for error. This tends to breed a perfectionism that is thinly disguised as hyper-disciplined work ethic.

The psychological ecosystem surrounding the legal profession can reward rigid thinkers and can pain creative thinkers. Since there is zero room for any kind of error, I find that most lawyers have become highly reliant on their rational, analytical ability and have almost trained themselves to neglect their 'feeling' domain.

The questions that my friend from law school grappled with are the same riddles I hear from Escape members all the time:

- If not this, then what?

- If I'm not meant to be a lawyer, then what am I meant to be?

- If I don't do this, then what else am I qualified to do?

- If I leave this tribe of familiar faces and colleagues and acquaintances, how else do I find my place in the world?

These are tough questions but you cannot know the answers to them without experimenting a little.

Therefore the goal should not be to 'know' the answers before you leap, but to be prepared to go on a discovery process, listening to all aspects of yourself (not just your rational mind) along the way.

Instead of placing the expectation upon yourself to magically 'know' all the serendipitous opportunities that are bound to cross your path along the way – instead of expecting yourself to 'know' what it is that you are going to do – a more efficient first step might be finding a coach. A coach can help you map the rest of the discovery process.

In the first chapter, we talked about impasse, and the 'stuck' feeling that can come with being at an existential intersection. In the second chapter, we looked at the importance of mentally preparing yourself for transition and becoming aware of the barriers that you might use to rationalise your way out of making a change.

In this chapter, we will look at one of the key tools that can be used to catalyse our way through an impasse. We will look at how coaches can be used to gain clarity and increased self-awareness.

AN INTRODUCTION TO COACHING

When we seek advice, often what we're seeking is validation. Deep down, we already know exactly what we need to do.

Often, when Escape members came to me looking for advice, I would refer many of them onto coaches. A coach is a skilled professional who works to help clients reach a specific goal in their personal or professional development. The coaching process is designed to enable clients to maximise their potential in specific areas that are most important to them.

Typically, a coach helps you to identify your goals, assists you with observations and insights that raise your self-awareness, and helps you to discover your own solutions and tactics for change. They also help you to track your progress and hold you accountable to your declarations for growth.

It is worth noting that coaches are not clinicians and should refer anyone with mental health problems to a trained specialist. For those who are suffering from actual depression the first route of support is their GP, who will refer them to clinical help.

Coaches are not therapists. Therapy deals with healing pain or conflict within an individual or relationships, where the focus is often on improving overall psychological functioning and dealing with emotional health. Coaching supports personal and professional growth based on a declaration of specific actionable outcomes. Coaching is future focused.

Coaches are not consultants. While individuals or teams retain consultants for their expertise in a given area, coaching assumes that individuals and teams can find their own solutions, with the coach there to provide supportive approaches and frameworks.

Coaches are not mentors. A mentor provides wisdom and guidance based on their own experience. While mentoring can include coaching, the coaching process itself does not include advising or counselling – instead, coaching focuses on helping individuals to reach their own objectives and to find their own answers.

SKEPTICISM SURROUNDING COACHES

I used to be fundamentally opposed to coaches. While at Escape, I received a slew of emails from random people trying to sell fluffy coaching programs and 'get rich quick' schemes. I enjoyed protecting our members from what was essentially spam.

This made me wary of anyone who called themselves a 'coach'. I've always approached career coaches the same way that I approach real estate agents and used car salesmen – if I can avoid them, I will.

However, meeting some very intelligent and capable coaches changed my mind, along with meeting Escape members who blatantly needed a trained professional to help them plan their transition. After meeting a few truly excellent coaches, I began to soften my judgments on what I soon realised I knew very little about.

Charly Cox was one of those truly excellent coaches. Her story has always fascinated me. She spent seven years working in Africa, where in addition to freelancing, she went on to found and grow her own communications company in Sierra Leone.

After starting the company with only $700, Charly grew it without outside investment to create an in-house multi-national team and a sizeable turnover, with clients including member agencies of the United Nations, Oxfam and British Airways.

She went on to train in coaching and now works in leadership development as a coach, trainer and speaker. I asked her for the advice that she would give those who might find themselves 'stuck'.

"Our heads are very noisy, complicated places, and we beat ourselves up a lot for 'not knowing' the answer," she says.

"People come to coaching because they yearn for something to change and feel like some help would get them there faster. At the root of everything is an emotional driver, and so I work with clients to help them to get clarity about what's driving them forward and what's holding them back. Fundamentally it's about helping people to be more authentically themselves."

"There's a saying that we can do amazing things when we just get out of our own way, and I like to think I help clients to do that. We clear out all of the noise made by the little voices of fear that tell us why we can't, and we turn up the volume on the intuition we've been ignoring that tells us we know, deep down, that we can. And then we set goals and get cracking."

"Just as you wouldn't think it weakness to use a hammer instead of your own hand to bang a nail into a wall, so you shouldn't see yourself as inadequate if you use a coach to get you to your goal," Charly explained. "Wouldn't it be a relief to say what you think more often, and not what you think other people want you to say?"

WHAT DOES A COACH
ACTUALLY DO?

Rikke Hansen is another coach who changed the way that I see the coaching industry. She's an internationally recognised expert and coach for career change and entrepreneurship based in London. She has worked with over 500 clients, been a business owner for over eight years and comes from a background in HR for Morgan Stanley, Shell and Citigroup.

She answered a few questions for me, the first of which was: what is it that a coach actually *does*?

"Anybody can do a weekend course in Slough and call themselves a 'coach'," Rikke warned. "The difference with the way I work is that I've got a background in HR plus over eight years of career change advisory experience."

So what is it that *you* uniquely do? I asked her.

"I help mid-career professionals discover what they *really* want to do, so they can refocus, change careers or start their own business," Rikke explained. "I draw out and identify what's truly unique about my clients – their personality, interests, story and skills – and "translate" that into careers or businesses on their terms."

Like a management consultant for someone's life or career, I thought. A consultant to help people exit the prisons they construct for themselves. A coach helps you to realign your current self with your ideal future self. By forcing you to stay accountable to your goals, a coach can be a crucial ally in clarifying your values and aligning your career with your dreams.

WORKING ON YOUR LIFE, NOT IN IT

One of my favourite business books is *The E-myth Revisited*. It talks about the importance of systems and separating yourself from the business, which is often what separates lifestyle businesses from scalable businesses.

The main lesson that I took away from it is the importance of working *on* your business instead of *in* it. When you have a strategy, it fundamentally changes the nature of how you design the operations and systems driving the business activity. This exponentially increases the effectiveness of the operations and therefore the very nature (and results) of the business itself.

Similarly, I find that when Escape members are thinking about career change, they often focus on the specifics of what's right in front of them instead of taking time to zoom out on the bigger picture. What a coach does is help you work on your life instead of in it.

A coach helps you to create a strategy for your life – one that you can't always see yourself when you're *in* your life.

Charly talks about how a career that feels right is one that aligns with your values. However, when you're in the midst of career change, it's difficult to see the forest for the trees. It's hard to remember what your values are when you're busy figuring out how to make things work financially.

This is why a coach can help you to separate the emotional task of figuring out what you want to do from the logical task of figuring how you can make that happen.

Charly says, "We are so conditioned to believe that we should be able to do everything by ourselves that hiring a coach may feel like admitting weakness or failure. I recently heard someone say that a coach is just a tool to get you where you want to be, and I love that idea."

When I was a teenager and learning to drive, I remember one thing that a driving instructor said to me that always stuck. I was inching the car between two cars parked very closely together. There was little space on either side of my car.

"Focus on the space that you're moving into, instead of the things blocking you," the instructor said. "If you focus on what you could crash into, you'll look at that, and you'll lose your focus and you're more likely to crash. Just focus on where you're trying to get towards."

Our minds are trained to spot the potential dangers (especially so if you're a lawyer), but focusing on those dangers doesn't actually help us to get to where we want to get to. In my opinion, the important thing to focus on is where you want to get to.

I've mentioned Rob Archer, a career psychologist that we often work with at Escape. At one event, he asked a very powerful question: "What does good look like?"

He said that with career change, we often let things like the loss of a monthly pay cheque, and the logistics take precedence. Forget that for now, he says. For now, zoom out. "What does your ideal look like? Paint it out clearly."

Focus on what you would be moving towards. Then figure out the rest.

"In a year's time, what does your ideal self look like? What values are more important than anything else?"

These were the questions that great coaches help you to answer. You already know your responses. A coach can help you to bring them into the forefront of your consciousness.

WHAT TO LOOK FOR IN A COACH

Escape members often ask what they should be looking for when selecting a coach. I often tell them to take advantage of the free consultation that most coaches typically give, so that they can ask themselves the following questions:

- Do we share similar values?

- Do I respect them on an intellectual level?

- Can I connect with them on an emotional level?

- Am I ready to commit to this process with this person?

- Do I feel comfortable opening up to them and sharing details and information about my career?

Coaching is an extremely personal process and is therefore an extremely personal decision, based on the unique interaction and chemistry that you may or may not develop with any given coach.

The specific elements that I take into consideration when looking for a good coach can often be gauged in the free initial consultation that most coaches offer.

CREDIBILITY

Some coaches are unlicensed while others have qualifications and certificates from coach training schools. However, badges don't necessarily signify excellence and excellence doesn't necessarily come with badges.

How you gauge credibility is up to you but personally I have found that I trust coaches who I can admire intellectually and who possess refreshingly original insights.

STRUCTURE

Your coach should ask you what your short and long-term goals are and what you want to achieve during your time together. The coach should help you to see the big picture but also keep you accountable to a weekly plan.

If your coach doesn't help you to set any goals, and your sessions with them simply fall into a circular discussion pattern, that's a red flag.

HONESTY

Ask the coach to keep you accountable. You need someone who isn't afraid to have tough conversations with you about your progress. While your coach will often rely on you to set your own pace, you want to know that in a few months' time, you will be at a different place.

INSPIRATION

The best coaches should lift you up and help you to articulate and reach what the best version of yourself looks like. Find a coach that gives you the feeling of being invincible (not invisible). A great coach should give you confidence and inspire you to work hard on reaching your goals.

INSIGHT

A great coach should be able to read you and to challenge you where necessary without making you feel threatened. They should make you aware of how realistic your goals are and what your blind spots are.

COMMUNICATION

You should always feel like you are able to contact your coach and to get an adequate response within a reasonable timeframe. Make sure that you clarify how often your coach intends to communicate with you and that this fits with your own personal preferences.

COACHES

These coaches are all London-based practitioners who we have often engaged with at Escape the City. I wouldn't list them here if I didn't believe in them myself (by the way, there is no affiliate deal or marketing going on here).

- Rob Archer: http://www.thecareerpsychologist.com/
- Charly Cox: http://charlycox.com
- Rikke Hansen: http://www.careeronyourterms.com/
- John Morgan: http://jpmorganjr.com
- Phil Bolton: http://www.lessordinaryliving.com

WHAT COACHES LOOK FOR IN A COACH

PHIL BOLTON:
"From my perspective an effective coach needs:

- To develop a clear structure and set of objectives for the engagement which support the client's agenda and define the outcomes clearly;
- To operate ethically and be clear on what coaching is and the limits of their ability;
- To be able to build trust and create an inspiring and strategic partnership for addressing the objectives."

CHARLY COX:

"TRAINING, TRAINING, TRAINING! Yes there are some instinctively great coaches, but no-one is harmed by a little training, and I'd say that people should be looking for coaches who trained with training schools affiliated with the International Coach Federation (ICF) or the European Mentoring and Coaching Council (EMCC). Ideally you want a coach who has completed more than one type of training, and someone who is continually refreshing their training.

So someone who trained once, a decade ago, might be excellent, but I'd personally prefer someone who continues to learn and is committed to that. It protects us from complacency. This is a personal opinion though. Most importantly a good coach must maintain confidentiality and be impartial. They shouldn't play expert, should abide by the ethical standards of the ICF/EMCC (http:// coachfederation.org/ethics/) and should NEVER give you advice."

How do you spot an ineffective coach? Giving advice is an alarm bell. If you suspect that your coach is attached to an idea (their idea) and trying to persuade you to do something, that's a sign that they've wandered off the ethical path. Again, check out their training.

There are lots of former consultants now rebranded as coaches, usually a 'something-coach' like a 'social media coach', and equally lots of people who are essentially mentoring. There's nothing wrong with consulting or mentoring – there's a lot right with it – but it's not coaching.

For me it's about integrity. Did they give you a free sample session? Did you feel a hard sell during it? A coach should be unattached full stop, not just during the coaching but during the enrolling and completing processes too. Coaches are as much doing as being. We're modelling for our clients (not in a perfect/pedestal/expert way), in a human way.

Our clients come to us to help them overcome fear and stand firmly in their values/confidence. Fundamentally they come for greater awareness. If we ourselves are standing in scarcity trying to 'snare' clients, what does that say about our own awareness of ourselves?

Rikke Hansen:
"It's important they are not just someone who has done a weekend course in Slough or only done their own escape and then think that's it (this is about your clients, not you!). For career changers specifically, it's really key that the coach/expert is able to help the client nail down what their career "problem" actually is as early as possible (i.e. how much of a career change do they need and why).

It's also important that the coach/expert is able to spot the difference between the person with potential in many areas who does not need more ideas but rather needs help to nail down the best option and get started; and the client who really struggles to come up with ideas and wonders if they are even qualified to do anything else. They need very different approaches and methodologies (the ignorance of which indicates an inexperienced or ineffective coach).

But the proof is really in the pudding – does the advice get results (when the client takes action) and does it fast-track them and help them avoid all of the classic pitfalls of the career change arena. Also, does the client feel that the coach/expert actually "gets them" on a personal level with all of their quirks, gifts and issues – that's key in order to establish the level of trust and credibility that creates the true magic and tailored solutions!"

JOHN MORGAN:
"A good coach is someone who shows you parts of yourself that not only were you not able to see, but that you didn't want to see. They create a space for you to become more of who you are. I also like this quote from Daniel Coyle's book 'The Talent Code":

"There are great coaches of behaviour and great coaches of knowledge, but there's a third type of great coach. These are mysterious types who often go overlooked, because what they do doesn't look like coaching. It looks more like magic. Because these people have the ability to alter someone's destiny in the time it takes to eat lunch. They aren't about how or why – they're completely, utterly about whom. Their core skill is to see someone in a way that they don't yet see themselves; to give their lives a larger narrative, sense of belief, a higher purpose. You might call them a Soul Coach.""

HENRY'S STORY:
"REFRAMING RISK"

I left law because I hated the hours, the stress, the pressure and increasingly, myself.

There was no silver bullet that made up my mind. Just an increased cumulative feeling that I was wasting my time and was unlikely to ever be happy doing this.

I have started a company called Adventure Yachting. (adventureyachting.co.uk). It's an agency business. I find amazing sailing trips from all over the world and market them to interested parties. It goes beyond just sailing though and I can arrange skiing, mountaineering, diving, photography, research, surf, conservations trips etc. The idea is to appeal to more people than the standard sailing crowd and to use sailing boats to take people to some of the world's must stunning and extreme locations. Places that you cannot reach except by boat.

I financed my move away from law by being a lawyer. That sounds facetious, but the saving grace of private practice is that it pays well. I knew I was leaving about a year before I left. I worked out my finances and saved as much as I could. I had bought a flat two years previously. This had left me broke at the time but proved really valuable when it came to leaving.

The main person I spoke to about the decision to leave was the life coach Phil Bolton. He was great and made the whole transition seem possible in my head. He broke down a load of the mental barriers that I had. He was worth every penny.

A lot of the work with my life coach was spent breaking down my natural aversion to risk. You need to keep 'risk' in perspective though. Eventually, it became clear that the biggest risk to me was staying in law. It was killing me ever so slowly!

I was never a fussy perfectionist lawyer, but all lawyers are like this to a degree. You have to be. One of the big things about leaving law is realising that the rest of the world does not adhere to the values and perfection obsession you find in a law firm. You will need to get used to this. Attention to detail is always going to be a useful trait to have though.

I spoke to the managing director of a large sailing company and asked him how he would suggest leaving law. He said come and work for him. So I did. I spent ten months that year in Greece skippering yachts.

After that I returned to the UK with a load of experience and ideas about the business that I wanted to start. I formally started the business last May, but had done a load of work in the run up to that. I have done some legal work, as a contractor, during this period to bring in some cash and fund the business while it gets traction.

When I was first getting started I went to a load of start-up events, including Escape the City's brilliant Start-Up MBA. This was so helpful in getting you into the mindset of a successful start-up entrepreneur. It is also great for reducing your chances of failure, or at least reducing your losses in the event that you do.

* * *

IN A NUTSHELL

» When we are finding our way out of impasse, we need to use our minds, our hearts, and our gut to make decisions about our next steps. However, in a high-pressure environment like law, using the mind and neglecting the other faculties is often the dominant mode that is encouraged. Therefore, trying to 'feel' your way through a decision may be especially challenging.

» A coach can help you to realign your current self with your ideal future self. Like any industry, there are a lot of charlatans out there, but there are also some very intelligent and invaluable coaches.

» You're not meant to have all the answers straight away, before even embarking upon the journey – you're meant to discover as you go. A coach can help you map the journey.

FURTHER RESOURCES

» Archer, Rob. "Career Paralysis – Five Reasons Why Our Brains Get Stuck Making Career Decisions." *Slide Share*. 4 Sept. 2010. Web. 16 Nov. 2014. <http://www.slideshare.net/robarcher/career-paralysis-pt-1-five-reasons-why-our-brains-get-stuck-making-career-decisions-5128274/>

» Bolton, Phil. "How To Get Focused And Find Fulfilling Work" *Less Ordinary Living*. 21 Sept. 2011. Web. 10 Nov. 2014. <http://www.lessordinaryliving.com/blog/how-to-get-focused-and-find-fulfilling-work/>

» Coyle, Daniel. The Talent Code: Greatness Isn't Born. It Is Grown. Arrow, 2010. Print.

» Gerber, Michael E. The E-Myth Revisited: Why Most Small Businesses Don't Work And What To Do About It. HarperCollins, 1995. Print.

» Hansen, Rikki. *"Career Change: How Do You Start?"* Online Video. Youtube. 22 May. 2013. <https://www.youtube.com/watch?v=5XnNlRwOezQ>

» Morgan, John. *"How To Find Your Passion"* Online Video. Youtube. 19 Jun. 2011. <https://www.youtube.com/watch?v=5XnNlRwOezQ>

EXERCISES

These are suggestions directly quoted
from coach Charly Cox:

» *Take a day off and go for a long walk, or sit in a coffee shop. Allow your natural creativity the chance to come out and play, and doodle in a notebook for no particular reason. Don't set any goals for the day, just fiddle about. And notice how you feel. Notice and jot it down. Committing thoughts to paper seems to be a great way of setting a powerful intention, and so however scrappy your notes are, scribble!*

» *Your values paint a powerful picture of what being in your element would look like. Write a list of your values and then choose four or five and create sub lists of what each value means to you.*

» *Ask five people to tell you the 10 things they think you're really great at. Paint it loud and proud and don't brush it off. In there lies the clue to what you'd be good at: you might not be doing it in your day job.*

HOW I ESCAPED: JIM'S STORY

"I am now the only Dad that makes it to every sports match for my son."

BragItUp.com was inspired by a 'Dragon's Den' conversation with some friends. I had had an idea that I should launch a website that tracked down the best online deals, and then these would be released to our readers. It came about during a particularly quiet week at home when I wanted to keep myself busy. So I researched setting up a website, potential competitors, creating a database and finding deals.

Since leaving university my wife had always worked in PR. When she gave birth to our son she somehow found herself picking up clients whilst in coffee shops and walking the pram! Having thought about what we could charge and how many clients we could expect to take-on, we realised that we could set up our own agency. Bearing in mind this was in 2006, so pre-crash, when there was a lot of business optimism and entrepreneurialism.

I am a saver by nature, and so even having bought a house in Wimbledon the year before, we had enough to see us through the first six months (even if none of our clients paid us!).

The only person I spoke to about the move away from the law was my wife, as she was the only person to be directly affected by it. She was totally supportive and we both realised it was a 'now or never' moment.

We first set up our PR agency, Blunt Communications, and BragItUp.com came approximately a year and a half afterwards. Whilst my law experience was useful in setting up a corporation and for our accounts, it was actually fairly detrimental in some aspects.

Whilst legal emails to clients at the law firm would be very formal, for Blunt Communications and BragItUp.com, clients would expect less formality. This was a necessity where building relationships, trust and being able to sell a client to a journalist, were more important than, for example, email etiquette.

But my legal background is proving incredibly useful where I can cast my eye over contracts before they go to our clients' solicitors. This enables us to forewarn clients of potential issues and things to think about.

Pre-crash I think that there was a genuine 'can-do' spirit. Businesses seemed to have large budgets, mortgages were given out freely and I had seen the number of deals being pushed through at the law firm. For us, we never once thought that our businesses could not work. Whilst I am naturally cautious my wife and I were under 30 years old, so still young enough to be slightly daring!

Our families were totally supportive of our decision, although it took my mum about five years to stop asking when I was going back to the law. I think she liked to tell her friends at parties that I was a lawyer...

Our friends were also all very supportive, even slightly envious. I have a couple of friends who have said that they would love to do what I did, but either family commitments or lack of courage has dissuaded them.

My mum and dad always said "Go for it". Knowing that everyone is behind your decision does make things easier.

I left the law in April 2006, when our son was one year old. At that point we set up our PR and marketing agency, Blunt Communications. Work went well, with clients who were happy with our work and paid us on time (when you work for yourself you realise how important cashflow is!). Nine months later we moved to France for what we thought was a six month working holiday. It turned into three and a half years...

Before going to France I did a Google search for a house on a beach in the south of France with Wi-Fi. It came up with a property south of Perpignan, in a tiny fishing village called Port Vendres.

We lived, improved our French and our son went to French creche/school. Unfortunately our French experience also coincided with the global economic meltdown. Whilst we were still able to earn from our PR and marketing clients, work definitely slowed down. It was in this lull that I created BragItUp.com.

I had to research setting up a website, contacting retailers, finding out about affiliate networks, and finding potential advertisers.

After a few years in France we came back to England to enquire about enrolling our son in a school (in a few years' time). However, we were told that if we didn't return immediately, there was a strong chance our son would have to drop at least one school year on returning to England. So in the space of two weeks we gave notice, packed up all of our belongings, played a basketball tournament with our friends in Toulon, and came back to the UK.

Since returning to England Blunt Communications has really taken off, as we now have some incredibly talented clients. BragItUp.com is still rolling on, but last year we bought a house that needed (and still needs!) a huge amount of money spending on it. Unfortunately this was the profits from BragItUp.com that should have been reinvested.

Knowing what you were going to be paid every month provided great security. I miss chatting to some of the associates whom I worked with, although that is where Facebook comes in handy.

I absolutely have a better work/life balance now though. I am now the only Dad that makes it to every sports match for my son. And counting those 21 days of holiday allowance is no longer an issue.

However, the grass is not always greener. The security provided by the regular monthly pay cheque and steady progression to partnership is replaced by the chasing clients for payment of outstanding invoices. Irregular payments into the company account and keeping records of who owes how much is a constant.

Yet being able to see the direct impact your work has (both on your bank account and in the national press) is very satisfying. Taking my son and picking him up from school every day is absolutely fantastic as is watching all of his plays and sports matches.

My father had worked for Total Oil but then set up his own company with a business partner many years ago. So I always knew that working for yourself could be profitable and enjoyable.

* * *

[4]

FACING RESISTANCE

*"The problem with the world is that the intelligent people are
full of doubts, while the stupid ones are full of confidence."*

– Charles Bukowski

I sat in a café with a career counsellor who I had met through
an Escape event. We were discussing what we had noticed
among various corporate professionals who wanted to
change careers. She mentioned that she had trained in organisational behaviour, which was not surprising. She then
went on to reveal something that was.

"I'm also training in grief and bereavement counselling,"
she said. She went on to talk about how part of career change
involves a loss of identity, status, salary and routine.

"It's a grieving process that most people struggle with,"
she explained.

When we start to accept that this loss and grief is a natural
part of career change, we can start to understand why it is
that we resist it.

I have had countless discussions with Escape the City
members who want to make a change but are too scared to

do so because of what they think their family, friends, or peers might think.

They not only grapple with their own internal resistance ('How will I make money? Who do I even think I am to change careers? Am I being selfish?') but also struggle to reconcile themselves with the resistance posed by others ('Why are you giving up such a great job? Are you mad? How do you propose to build a new career at this age?').

WHY RESISTANCE OCCURS

People resist change for many reasons but the common source tends to be fear: the fear of change, the fear of our ability to adapt, the fear of the unknown. These fears can be linked to the loss and grief that will come with the change – whether it is colleagues, the office environment, or the salary – or the loss of self-esteem, status, and feeling of peer approval.

"I like the way people react to me when I tell them that I'm a barrister," one Escape member said to me once. *"I feel like they listen to what I'm saying because there's a perception that I'm smart."*

Katherine, who I mentioned earlier, adds:

"In my experience, I have felt the loss of the natural credit you seem to get when you tell people you are a lawyer or the initial 'wow' response that is surprisingly common. But I've also found that suddenly having to describe who you are and what you do is much harder.

Instead of a one word, all-encompassing descriptor you're left fumbling for something vague like 'I'm looking into this' or 'I'm trying my hand at this' if you haven't yet locked in your next career move," she explains. *"It can also take some time getting used to a new non-law title, and the new identity that comes with it. I've known a lot of people who continue to reference their previous identity as a lawyer when asked what they do, saying 'Well, I used to be a lawyer, but now I'm a...'*

There are potentially two kinds of resistance from other people: Resistance from others when you commit to a new job/path ("oh, you're not a lawyer anymore?"), or resistance from others when you're in a period of transition and not quite sure what you're doing yet.

In relation to the latter, how you "sell" your transition directly affects how people relate to it. If, in response to a question like "what are you doing now", you respond with doubt, uncertainty and unease, those emotions will be reflected back in the answers and opinions of the people you are talking to.

I noticed people who were going through a transition much more successfully than I (i.e., with less stress, doubt and uncertainty) had a really good way of marketing their transition to people who asked the inevitable "what are you doing now" question, with a very positive and exciting "pitch", backed with a lot of confidence. It is a variation of the "fake it until you make it" concept – if you speak confidently about what you're doing, you'll become more confident about it too – even in the face of resistance."

The resistance of others ruffles us when we are feeling doubtful within ourselves. During moments when I feel fragile, if someone says something negative towards me, it can leave me feeling terrible. During moments when I feel strong, if someone says something negative, I'm able to shake it off and know that it reflects more on them than it does on me.

The most practical way to rise above the negative voices of resistance is this: make your own voice stronger. The more you take action outside of your comfort zone, the more your comfort zone will expand. You don't have to do it all in one go – take small steps.

SELF-SABOTAGE

Rikke Hansen, who we met in the last chapter, talks about how mapping an escape route starts with working through self-sabotage:

"Self-sabotage results from a misguided attempt to rescue ourselves from our own uncomfortable feelings, rather than dealing with them. The problem is that rather than solving the problem or making those uncomfortable feelings go away, they actually get worse or intensify.

It can seem scary to get out of your comfort zone and decide to leave what you perceive as a safe job. However, I would suggest that the most empowering thing you can do in this new economy is to take full responsibility for your career by knowing what you really want, what you have to offer and what to call that in a way that makes you stand out from the crowd."

She talks about the common self-sabotage scenarios she sees at the early part of the career change process:

"ALL OR NOTHING"
A very common one is the "all or nothing" scenario – the belief that there is no point in even considering a career change unless it's a truly dramatic one, usually involving lots of re-training, certifications and a drastic salary cut, like going from being an investment banker to becoming a social worker.

"This belief can be really damaging since all it makes you do is focus on the sacrifices, time and effort it would take," Rikke explains. "However, a career change is rarely a case of all-or-nothing scenarios."

She adds, "More often than not, the process is about identifying exactly how much (or little) of a career change you really need or want AND ensuring you are both emotionally and intellectually fully onboard with the changes you want to make."

My friend felt like an idiot every time I tried to ask her what she might want to do instead of law. ("If I knew, I'd be doing it, wouldn't I?" I can hear her hiss.)

As Hansen explains – the first thing to do before mapping an escape route is to stop falling into all-or-nothing thinking (Job to No Job/Job to Building Our Business Full Time/ Accountant to Nurse/Lawyer to Journalist). It doesn't have to be that extreme and we don't have to do it all at once. Job ads can make us feel awful because we often don't feel like we have any of the skills they are advertising for (especially if we're planning a big career change).

Hansen also makes the point that with a number of her clients, a large percentage of people don't need that much of a career change. Instead, they need a new boss or a change of environment, as opposed to a new profession or job description. We may be well suited to our jobs – perhaps the context or environment is what does not work.

"EXTERNAL SEARCH FIRST"
Another trend that sabotages career changers right out of the gate is to start off the career change process by looking "externally" first.

"This only increases your feelings of shortfall," Rikke says. "A successful career change starts from the inside out and self-knowledge is key. So make sure you get clear about what you really want and what you have to offer before seeking external input and opinion."

She articulates what I often see with our Escape members. "There are also a lot of professionals who get totally stuck in their unhappy career scenario because they don't know what else they can do 'with what they've got.' As if their past work history somehow dictates their future and the number of career options available to them."

Instead, she suggests, "Approaching the initial career change process by focusing on what you really want – irrespective of your past – is key here, as is effective communication of your unique selling points."

"TOO MUCH RESEARCH, NOT ENOUGH ACTION"
Another trend is isolation and turning your career change into a never-ending project as opposed to a reality. This ignores the fact that opportunities (especially those related to career change and entrepreneurship) most often come attached to people.

"Rather than hiding away behind your computer 'researching' excessively, you really need to get out and connect with people in the field you want to go into – by attending events, courses and especially social gatherings," Rikke argued.

She says that it is important to tell friends and contacts so they know what you are up to – if they don't, they can't help you. "It never ceases to amaze me how many of my clients' career changes kick into high gear when they actually start using networking as a key tool."

Katherine, who helped to edit this book and also recently left a big law firm, adds: "This can be a particularly common trap among lawyers. We are taught to research everything to the Nth degree before committing to it, we are often risk averse, and we have a pessimistic tendency (as we've already talked about). Lawyers tend to love plans, to-do lists and are well versed in extensive, never-ending research projects. This type of self sabotage is particularly relevant to a lawyer's transition."

A helpful framework to dealing with resistance can be found from Kurt Lewin, who emigrated from Germany to America during the 1930's and is often recognised as the founder of social psychology. Instead of trying to run away from resistance, it might be more useful to refer to what Lewin calls the Unfreezing and Change/Transition stages.

UNFREEZE, CHANGE, REFREEZE

The Kurt Lewin model of change forms the basis of many other more modern change models. While much has changed since this theory was originally presented in 1947, it is still very relevant and useful today. This three-stage theory of change is commonly referred to as Unfreeze, Change, Freeze (or Refreeze).

STAGE 1: UNFREEZING
This stage involves moving towards motivation for change. Without the motivation to change, change does not happen. In that sense, this stage is about getting ready to change: reaching an understanding that change is necessary. It's also the stage where we get ready to move away from our comfort zone.

Motivation to make the change often comes easier when we feel that change is necessary and urgent. This stage is about weighing up the pros and cons and deciding if the positives of change outweigh the negatives.

STAGE 2: CHANGE – OR TRANSITION
Lewin did not see change as an event but as a process, called transition – the inner movement or journey made in reaction to a change. As we make necessary changes, this second stage happens as we are 'unfrozen' and move towards a new way of being.

This can be the hardest stage as people can be unsure or fearful. It is during this stage that people learn about the realities of the change and need time to understand and adapt.

Coaching can be a useful tool here, as well as anticipating that mistakes will be part of the process. Role models can also be useful, or reading stories of those you wish to emulate. It can also be helpful to keep a clear picture of the desired change and benefits in order to keep track of the ideal outcome from the change process.

STAGE 3: FREEZING (OR REFREEZING)
While Lewin refers to this stage as freezing, a lot of people refer to it as 'refreezing', referring to establishing stability after changes have been made, accepted and become the new norm – there are new relationships and routines formed.

Since change has only become more inevitable and things seem to be increasingly fluid, this phase cannot be viewed as a fixed, permanent phase. It is simply the stage before a new 'unfreezing' process begins.

However, Lewin termed this phase a 'refreezing' to express concern that the desired change continues as opposed to people simply going back to what they were doing before.

Knowing these stages is useful because you can identify which stage you're in, and how there is a natural progression towards refreezing.

The clue to overcoming resistance is understanding that you cannot avoid resistance, but you can manage it.

Resistance does not indicate that change is bad or that the past has been a failure. Change is rarely smooth and linear – typically, you can take five steps forward, a few steps back, a few more steps forward, one more back, and so on.

We can see through Sam's story that change can be scary even when it is necessary. However, it becomes less scary when we can map some kind of route through unchartered territory, which often involves becoming aware of broader context.

SAM'S STORY (CONT'D): "SACRIFICES"

The biggest sacrifice that I had to make whilst working as a lawyer was sacrificing my principles about the type of person that I want to be, and the type of person that I always thought I had been. I'd always considered myself to be an interested, engaged and willing contributor – a portfolio guy: trying new things, enjoying opportunities and generally living for the moment.

Once working as a corporate lawyer, all of this disappeared. I was working a lot of the time, and I always seemed to be working on the same things, or in the same fashion, or with the same conventions. Everything was very static and well-established. Everything had a set process and the smallest deviation from standard practice took an awful lot of doing.

The hierarchy and bureaucracy were mind-numbing. There's no doubt that this is symptomatic of the fact that I was working for a huge corporate law firm. And to be clear, I don't think for a second that this way of working is wrong – after all, it's a well-established corporate player for a reason. But it was wrong for me, it wasn't what I wanted, and I felt entirely unfulfilled.

The longer I worked in corporate law, the more opportunities I missed and the more I became a walking, talking re-run of the same, stale conventions. I was always caught up working on things that I had almost no interest in, that I had no passion for, and that had no realistic prospect of leading me anywhere that I wanted to get to. I was always busy and it felt like I was never really delivering anything! And worst of all I was always cancelling on friends, as though it was acceptable. It's not; it's rude.

Whatever it was that I wanted to be, I wasn't. And why? It was because my job restricted me (both in time and in substance) from engaging with the things that excited me. A lot of my time was wound up with being in the office (regardless of whether there was work to do). When I wasn't in the office, I was so bored and numb from my job that I lacked the energy and enthusiasm to focus on the things that did excite me.

I found myself disinterestedly careering along on a path that was doing nothing for me, and time just kept on ticking by. Worst of all, I didn't feel like I was learning anything. I was well and truly stuck. Bored, demotivated and demoralised.

My life was slipping away from me. And with every day in a law firm that slowly sapped my drive and ambition, I sacrificed my principles more and more. This sacrifice served as an emphatic fillip to inspire me to do other things.

It was abundantly clear to me that what I wanted from my professional experience and what I wanted from my personal life were both incompatible with the culture and aspirations of my corporate law firm. In terms of this disconnect, I'm not talking about a heavy workload or committing to unsociable hours – I get it, if you want to achieve highly then you have to work very hard.

The disconnect was in terms of what the firm needed from me and what I wanted from, and for, myself. All the firm could give me was money and stability. But that wasn't what I wanted for myself. I wanted to be enthused, to be interested in what I was doing, and to be motivated by and committed to the projects that I was working on.

* * *

IN A NUTSHELL

» A grieving process alongside career change is perfectly normal. The key is to accepting resistance and anticipating it instead of trying to avoid or demonise it. Resistance is a natural part of any transition. Change can be scary even when it is necessary.

» Self-sabotage can come in a number of forms: including the "all or nothing" scenario, looking externally first and turning your career change into a never-ending project as opposed to a reality.

» The Kurt Lewin model of change outlines three stages: unfreezing, change, and then freezing again. Becoming aware of an impasse indicates unfreezing; the change process itself can often be the most challenging; and freezing again refers to settling into your new arrangement, whatever that may be.

FURTHER RESOURCES

» *Brene Brown.* Web. <brenebrown.com>

» Lewin, K. "Frontiers in group dynamics. Concept, method and reality in social science; social equilibria." *Human Relations,* 1947, 1, 5-40

EXERCISES

» What resistance thoughts do you most commonly feel that stop you from actually making a career change? What systems can you put in place to challenge those thoughts?

» Who is going to resist the change in your life? Whose reactions will trigger you the most? Why are they behaving that way and how will you deal with them accordingly?

HOW I ESCAPED: EMMA'S STORY

"Lawyers, as a rule, do not use their intuition or gut feeling as this would go against the grain of being a lawyer. I found that re-engaging with this dormant resource enabled me to take 'risks' that I knew were instinctively right and I felt comfortable with."

I was a commercial property lawyer in the city and found that my daily life on the corporate treadmill was becoming less and less inspiring. I worked as a lawyer for a number of years (both in private practice and client side) and I always felt that something was missing in my life but couldn't quite put my finger on what I wanted to do. I felt that I was trapped in a well paid job with no other options available to me.

I was made redundant in 2009. While the decision to leave the law was made for me, I had been thinking about doing something else in the run up to the redundancy because I didn't want to turn into Dorian Gray. Eight months before I was made redundant, I took out unemployment insurance and this provided a financial safety net for me.

Looking back, I had never felt comfortable with being a lawyer and think I watched too much *LA Law* as a child and had a romanticised view of the profession. I was desperately unhappy and at my redundancy meeting, I had to hide the smile on my face: it was a total liberation for me and I felt my life was about to begin.

I would be lying if I said it was a completely smooth transition to where I am now – which transition is? In many respects, many people view redundancy as being 'fired' or you get the chop because you didn't quite make a grade. I did go through a period of self pity. Applying for 400 jobs with only two interviews as a result of my efforts did not help. However, I now know this was the universe telling me I was going down the wrong path and to escape the relentless rejection, I went travelling for a few months. I came back to the UK with the intent of moving abroad permanently.

Upon my return and even more rejected job applications later, I became very despondent and a friend suggested I see a careers coach to help me find my direction and purpose. This was the best thing I could have done, because it helped me reignite my dormant passion for photography and I ended up meeting my now business partner on a photography course. I wanted to be a photographer in my early teens but I decided to go down the academic route instead. Seeing a careers coach was an invaluable experience and it enabled me to have the courage to set up my business ventures and regain my shattered confidence.

I formed a photography business called 'Abitoffthemapp Photography' and set out to sell my images at art fairs, markets and entered photography competitions. It was a way to test public opinion about my work. It was a resounding success and I soon realised that I wanted to formally exhibit my work.

After doing some research, it became apparent that this was difficult unless you knew someone who owned a gallery or had connections in the industry. On the back of this, I decided to set up the 'London Photo Festival' to enable new and emerging photographers to exhibit their work free from evaluation and to bypass the formal gallery route. We are in our third year and are growing from strength to strength, exhibiting photographers from around the globe.

In August 2013, we set up a pop-up gallery called the 'London Photo Gallery'. We are now in the process of establishing a presence at international art fairs.

I do not regret training as a lawyer. My legal experience has helped me without a doubt but it can also be a little bit of a hindrance as you can overcomplicate matters and take things too seriously. Quite often, to think too long about doing a thing often becomes its undoing. I am also notoriously stubborn at asking for help and think I can do everything on my own, so when a friend suggested that I get a business partner I was quite reluctant (too much of a control freak!). But this was the best piece of advice that I was given because you cannot do everything on your own and other people bring different skill sets to the business which enable you to drive the business forward.

I now have what is referred to as a portfolio career. After accepting that I wouldn't make enough money from photography alone, I took on two part-time jobs which help to keep my bank manager happy. I work for myself and enjoy the flexibility and freedom that comes with this. I was so used to having one stable job, but the recession has actually shown me that I have so many more options. Above all, I am the happiest I have ever been and no longer have the fear on a Sunday evening about going to work on Monday.

Being a lawyer works for some people, it was just wasn't for me. Lawyers, as a rule, do not use their intuition or gut feeling as this would go against the grain of being a lawyer. I found that re-engaging with this dormant resource enabled me to take risks that I knew were instinctively right and I felt comfortable with.

The advice I would you to someone who is thinking about leaving the law is to do your research about your next move. Use your intuition and trust yourself. Get a business partner, business plan, mentor, and life or career coach. Network, network, network. Feel the fear and do it anyway. Don't take things personally – if something (or someone you are working with) isn't working, then usually there's a reason for it. Move on to something else.

Use your time wisely and learn from other people. Surround yourself with like-minded people. You can't do it all so concentrate on what you can do. Enjoy yourself: life really is too short to be stuck in a job that makes you unhappy. Stick to your own journey and don't pay any attention to what other people are doing.

* * *

[5]

EXPERIMENTING STRATEGICALLY

"The fastest way to change yourself is to hang out with people who are already the way you want to be."

—Reid Hoffman

Raglan is a surf town about an hour's drive from Auckland, New Zealand. On my last trip there, somewhere between the sea breeze and the rhythm of the waves, I started wondering why I hadn't told more stressed-out corporate prisoners to seek refuge in this peaceful part of the planet. Then I recalled that too much pleasure leads to a listless drift, a boredom that can often feel like a prison of its own.

As much as we complain about the demands that work can place on us, our egos enjoy feeling important. Whenever I've been on a project that requires me to work overtime, I've felt like my presence has more weight. Walking through fancy offices and shaking hands with fancy people can make you feel fancy by association.

When Escape members tell me that they feel busy but not productive, present but not there, it reminds me of how Alain de Botton describes the evenings of work junkies in

The Pleasures and Sorrows of Work:

"The challenge lies in knowing how to bring this sort of day to a close. His mind has been wound to a pitch of concentration by the interactions of the office. Now there are only silence and the flashing of the unset clock on the microwave. He feels as if he had been playing a computer game which remorselessly tested his reflexes, only to have its plug suddenly pulled from the wall. He is impatient and restless, but simultaneously exhausted and fragile. He is in no state to engage with anything significant."

Deep down, we all have a compass that tells us when we're heading in the wrong direction. A lot of the time, it's easier to ignore that compass, because we're too busy or fragile or exhausted to seriously entertain alternatives. Still, I've seen many Escape members reach a point when they become sick of the person that their ambition has turned them into.

SAM'S STORY (CONT'D): "BUILDING EXPERIMENTS"

I was phenomenally unproductive when working as a lawyer. Inevitably, this made me really miserable, as I had a real sense that I was wasting my time. High achievers are accustomed and programmed to work hard, execute and get things done. The fact that I had no motivation to do this anymore was alien to me, alien and dispiriting. I couldn't shake the feeling that I wasn't doing anything worthwhile professionally; it was horrific.

It became apparent to me that many of my peer group are the same. Everyone is always talking about when they're going to be found out for not having done any work. I was consistently thinking to myself – how on earth have I spent 12 hours in the office today but feel like I've only completed about 40 minutes worth of work.

I read a brilliant line from an Esc member recently: "I always seem to be working but I never seem to deliver anything." That's exactly how I felt.

I had to start focusing on doing other things – projects outside of work, planning trips and setting up start-ups. When working on those things, I was ridiculously productive – and I loved working on them. I already knew I had to leave but the juxtaposition of the two worlds that I was occupying – one where so much was meaningless and where I always felt I was treading water, and the other where I was so charged, setting tough targets and surpassing them – made this crystal clear to me. There was no greater impetus for change than that contrast. Here were things that I was passionate about and that I was making real progress with in a direction that I wanted to go. So why on earth was I spending so much of my time on other things that didn't satisfy me in anywhere near the same way? At work I was always thinking about the opportunities that I was missing. And if you miss too many opportunities, at some point you'll run out of them.

The most important thing for me is to be happy. Working in law, I was categorically not happy and my disappointment and frustration with my career was so pervasive that they impacted the rest of my life. I attempted to completely separate my professional life from everything else. This in itself was a personal disappointment as I felt that surely the ideal is that you do enjoy your work, that you do want to talk about it, and that you do want to put everything into making a success of it. These were not sentiments that I felt about my work. I tried to switch off completely once out of the office and I would attempt to quickly skirt over any conversation about jobs. I didn't want to talk about it, because I wasn't interested in my job and I wasn't proud of myself for doing what I was doing.

* * *

RUNNING AWAY

When you feel like you might be going down the wrong road, a common instinct is to U-turn – I have seen countless people chuck in their high-flying jobs without thinking about what comes next. What typically happens once the pressure has been lifted – once the job has been quit – there is a vast emptiness. Suddenly, they don't have to be anywhere. The empty schedule can be terrifying.

So, more often than not, they travel. They go absorb beautiful parts of our planet and they feel their spirits lift and they connect with whatever they felt disconnected from before – that sense of wonder and beauty, that reminder of a universe beyond their former daily routine.

Once the high of the travel ends, there's a comedown, because now they have to deal with all the things that they previously avoided. Before, they were too busy working. Then they were too busy travelling. Now… there remains nothing to distract them from themselves.

Alternatively, even if they choose to stay in their home city without a plan in place, time away from the pace of regular work can be easily wasted. I remember one Escape member who took six months off only to spend the entire time at home playing video games. He returned to the same job six months later even more depressed than he was when he initially left.

Running away isn't the solution because to know what we are going to do next, we need external feedback that can only be gained through meeting new people and trying new experiments.

Members often said to me (just like my friend did too), "If I knew what I wanted to do, I'd be doing it!" But you don't know what you don't know. The point of experimentation is to dispel your own fantasies and preconceptions about new areas and to build your information database of what career might work best for you.

Getting out into the natural environment can help to kickstart a new thought process, but being in Raglan reminded me that while running away off the grid can give renewed energy to begin career construction, escapism will never be a construction in itself.

ADVICE FROM ESCAPE THE CITY CO-FOUNDER ROB SYMINGTON

You are not going to suddenly "just know" what you are meant to do with your life in a searing moment of clarity on your commute to your job. You cannot think or analyse your way to a passion.

Passions are grown through inquisitively pursuing interests, getting good at things, and making yourself useful to the world. Through the hard work of DOING different things you will find yourself drawn towards certain activities and, if you are self-aware and keep acting with purpose, you can BECOME passionate about new things.

No one really knows what they are doing when they start, they just started. The belief that you're "just not one of those people who has a clear passion or clear interests" is rubbish. "You might be thinking "that's all very well for Rob to be clear on his mission, but I haven't got a clue about mine".

A couple thoughts on this front:

1) I wasn't clear on my mission when I left my consulting job five and a half years ago and started working on a wild idea to help people escape unfulfilling careers – I just followed my interests towards something that I felt was worthwhile.

2) Your mission can change as often as you need it to; it is constantly evolving. Pick something you know you care about and start doing it – you'll get all the information you need about your values and your mission through forward action.

You aren't going to make your career change or start your business by thinking about it. You're going to do it by taking small steps in the direction of your goals. Don't have any goals yet? Don't worry.

Start taking small steps in lots of directions (without quitting your job) and see what you discover (about yourself and the world). The key is that you take actions – rather than living through hundreds of scary scenarios in your head.

If we were doctors treating you for "feeling stuck on your career change plans" our prescription would be as follows: stop the all or nothing thinking (rich/poor, happy/miserable, success/failure) and take the pressure off by leaving the actual resignation on the shelf for now. All you have to do is: Learn, Experiment, and Network.

Exposing yourself to new ideas (learning), new experiences (experimenting) and new people (networking) is the best way of opening yourself up to new possibilities. And you can do ALL of this without quitting your job.

Escapees often say they feel like fate is rewarding them for making the leap.

We think the reality is far more straightforward, they are simply doing the scary work of trying new things and, through that, discovering potential new paths.

WHAT IF I DON'T KNOW
WHAT TO DO?

This is a tough question and the heart of the struggle. You are most likely reading this because you don't actually know what to do. If you did, I think it is likely that you would already be moving towards that goal.

I loved gathering the stories for this book and they offer so many perspectives on how to work through the process of leaving the law. However, they are all "success" stories in that they are told from "successful escapees" who are looking back on how they left the law and moved into something more fulfilling.

So while it is easy to perceive the stories as being told from people who always knew what to do, or always had a plan, I thought it might be helpful to elaborate a bit more on the question that plagues all of us at some point or another.

In his book *Not Knowing: The Art of Turning Uncertainty Into Opportunity*, Steven D'Souza writes about how to see the opportunity in times when you lack conventional knowledge. He gave a talk at Escape and explained how change and transformation begin in the dark – in a mother's womb, in the soil before the roots of a plant push their way to the surface.

"Darkness is the place of the unknown; the place past the edge of your knowledge; a place that is full of possibilities if you can embrace it," recalls Escape member Janine Esbrand, who attended his talk.

Another guest blog post on Escape the City, written by Ethan Crane, asked this question: *How Can I Make the Escape From My Career Less Terrifying?*

Crane writes:

"The reason we stay in full-time careers is for the feeling of security. If nothing else our pointless jobs give us a salary each month, and that salary means we have somewhere to live and the means to entertain ourselves.

But security is not really security. It's financial security, perhaps. But it is not psychological security, because your boss' ability to say, 'we're letting you go' at any time they please, without warning, is the cattle-prod that keeps you working late, taking on more work and becoming stressed and fatigued.

Living with part-time or freelance work for money is less secure. But it is actually living. Not having a regular income each month can be worrying, but not nearly as worrying as you might imagine. I have been worrying about my varying monthly income for 15 years now, and when I'm not worrying I listen to my fellow self-made careerists own worries about money. Year after year, as they continue to find time for the work they really love.

There will never be complete security in a self-made career. We should not want there to be. A certain level of insecurity is necessary to be in a position to take opportunities that arise. In a full-time career you don't see the opportunities because you are not able to take them."

As we've already discussed, it is perfectly fine not to know what to do and it isn't going to come to you in a moment of clarity – you have to work towards it. Matt Trinetti, an Escape team member and close friend, writes about how he landed his job at Escape the City, in an essay called, "How Can I Land My Dream Job?" He outlines how finding our new answers is a process more than a simple overnight evolution:

"You don't get closer to a dream job by wishing and hoping, by perusing job boards (ironic given that's part of our business), or by machine-gun firing off your resume to any company with a pulse. You land a dream job by doing things that matter to you, through action. By leaving the building and getting to know people who care about the same things you care about."

Another Escapee, Jane Pendry, author of 'Edible Rambles' food blog, talks about how she now deals with the question, "What do you do for a living?" in a recent article for Escape the City titled "How to Explain the 'Next Steps', When the 'Next Steps' are Unknown". Pendry explains:

"This transitional period has provided me with the perfect petrie dish to test various explanations. I tried saying 'I don't know', but this response, no matter how true it might be, often halts the conversation completely. I also tried to explain that I was navigating a career transition, but this always invited the question: 'a transition from what to what?'

I have now settled on a kind of 'elevator pitch', covering a broad business concept, focusing more on my unique selling points, and an explanation of how I want to spend my time day to day. This leaves the space open for discussion while providing a concise answer so that the conversation can move on."

INGREDIENTS OF FULFILLING WORK

Often people aren't searching for endless pleasure – they're searching for meaning. The ideal, it seems, is not to pursue endless pleasure but is to experience a professional occupation that combines what you love, what you're good at, and what pays well.

Finding this can involve creating space in our lives to experiment, so that we can find out what makes us feel what Mihaly Csikszentmihalyi calls 'flow' – a state of complete absorption with the activity at hand. Members often think they need to 'find their passion' in order to be happy but often what they're actually looking for is flow.

Turning flow into a well-paid career is rarely an easy process. Sometimes that journey has to involve doing the wrong thing first so that we know how to spot the right thing later, as author and careers thinker Daniel Pink says:

"One source of frustration in the workplace is the frequent mismatch between what people must do and what people can do. When what they must do exceeds their capabilities, the result is anxiety. When what they must do falls short of their capabilities, the result is boredom. But when the match is just right, the results can be glorious. This is the essence of flow."

In his book *Drive: The Surprising Truth About What Motivates Us*, Pink talks about the three things we need in order to find that match that's 'just right'.

Firstly, we need autonomy, or the power to have control over ourselves and our days. Many Escape members seem convinced that if they just had more pleasure in their life, they'd be happy. They think that they've chosen the wrong job, and that's what's making them unhappy. However, they have often chosen a perfectly suitable sector and role. What they're actually hungry for is more control over their time.

Secondly, we need mastery, or to keep getting better at something that's meaningful to us. Mastery is the eternal challenge; the ongoing competition with ourselves. Maybe it starts with flow – when you enjoy what you're doing, you have the patience required to develop competence. Competence breeds confidence: knowing that you're good at something makes you want to do it more.

The thing is, many members are either competent at skills that don't give them 'flow' or aren't willing to start at the bottom again in order to retrain and find that 'flow' in other areas. So to achieve mastery, they either need to make peace with having the skills they already have, or become willing to endure beginner's pain again.

Thirdly, Pink talks about purpose: the sense that what we do helps to serve something important beyond ourselves.

So how do you apply this to your own career construction?

CAREER REINVENTION CONCEPTS

I often find myself recommending the book *Working Identity: Unconventional Strategies for Reinventing Your Career*, by Herminia Ibarra, a professor of organisational behaviour at INSEAD. It provides a practical framework for integrating the ingredients of fulfilling work in your own life.

Ibarra talks about mid-career changers who want to escape numbing or boring work to find a more meaningful vocation. She explores 'figuring out how to transfer old preferences and values to a new and different context and how to integrate those with changing priorities and newly blooming potential.'

Her idea is that effective career change is about linking our deepest values with what we do. Ibarra talks about crafting experiments, shifting connections, and 'reinterpreting our life stories through the lens of the emerging possibilities.'

Ibarra talks about three intelligent ways to spend your time when you're looking to switch careers, which involve crafting experiments, shifting connections, and making sense. These are how you find your unique selling proposition – your 'what', as coach Rikke Hansen calls it.

1. Craft experiments

Ibarra urges career changers to stop trying to find the one true self – instead, she says, pay attention to the various possible selves you want to experiment with.

Realise that there is a limit to how much you can find out about yourself through introspection. Ask who you might become – what are the possibilities? Which among your various potential selves can you start to discover now? How? Put these into hypotheses then take action to prove or disprove those hypotheses.

Ibarra also encourages small wins rather than untested leaps. Projects can be valuable baby steps instead of big and serious problems like figuring out our entire life. She votes for extracurricular activities or parallel paths that can be done alongside the existing day job. Even just going to interviews and other networking events can be helpful.

She then says to take feedback from those actions to take stock of your reactions. After doing some of the above, you then start to decipher your enduring values and preferences, using your internal gauge – does it feel right? Can you see yourself doing this?

These are experiments, Ibarra argues. So surprising outcomes are expected. This is how you can learn what to embrace and what to avoid. Vary the experiments, so that you can compare and contrast results before selecting your options.

Leave room for serendipity, Ibarra says.

Here are some brief examples of how others have done it:

- Connor offered his services to a growing start up that had a great idea and began consulting with them on their future direction and strategy over beers every Tuesday night.

- Kara always suspected that she would love to be an event organiser and offered to volunteer for one of Auckland's best event venues on Saturdays to see how she found it.

- Sarah wondered whether she would enjoy being a writer, so she challenged herself to write one article a week on her private blog and tracked how she felt about completing this task.

- Nikki was passionate about health and wellbeing and in her spare time scoured food blogs learning about food photography, styling and recipe creation before launching her own site.

- Deanne, whose story we explore below, crafted her own experiment of going to a 10-weekend course in film production.

DEANNE'S STORY: "IT WASN'T A STUPID PIPE DREAM"

I'm not a risk-averse person by nature, which is probably why I was never cut out to be a lawyer. But I definitely got sucked into the single-minded corporate mindset that makes you feel like law is the only option and an alternative career would be madness. I was made to question my decision almost daily until I left and it was really hard sometimes to stick to my guns and not take the easy option. It was only when I found myself crying with relief the day I left that I realised what a huge weight had been lifted from my shoulders.

To prepare for my departure, I did a 10-weekend course in film production to see if I liked it. I loved it. I emailed everyone I knew to see if anyone could help get me work experience, and applied for lots of runner jobs at the BBC. But when I finished my training contract and left, I didn't have a job lined up, which was quite scary.

Once I decided to leave I saved up as much as I could for the remainder of my contract. Then I moved back up north and in with my long suffering parents so I didn't have to pay rent whilst trying to make the change.

Friends were very helpful at putting me in touch with people they knew who worked in the industry. Just having the support of my friends, family and boyfriend was also very important when making the leap.

It's not all been a bed of roses and you definitely have to accept that there are downsides to all careers. There are times when I've had to do shit jobs for terrible pay. I was poorer than most of my friends for a good few years. It's a tough industry and you have to have grit and determination to move up the ladder, which can be exhausting and frustrating. But the personal rewards are incredible if you're passionate about it. The fact I could always see an exciting future in my job made the tough times worth it – whereas the idea of being a partner at a law firm used to make me shudder.

Meeting a friend of a friend who had moved from law to a great career in film just crystallised the fact that this wasn't a stupid pipe dream, it was possible and realistic. This really gave me a boost.

* * *

2. SHIFT CONNECTIONS

Ibarra talks about building a new network – the importance of finding people who are what you wish to become. They can provide valuable support for the transition. Focus on distant acquaintances rather than close friends – they are likely to know different people from you and therefore different information. They are also less likely to feel betrayed or threatened by your change.

Look at the characteristics of the values and norms of those new peer groups. Find guiding figures who can act as mentors. Join communities of practice to pick up new skills and social norms. This will help to provide you with a secure base, from where you can slowly define and test a new self.

As obvious as it sounds, you are only ever hired by a *person*. New, exciting opportunities come from other *people* as opposed to job boards. At its best, networking is connecting with people with whom you have similar interests. Make sure to contact people instead of only doing research from behind your computer.

Use tools like Meetup.com to get out from behind your desk and interact with those who are working in the field that interests you.

Katherine offered some insights based on her and her peers' experience:

- Email people who are involved in an industry that you suspect you might like to break into and initiate a conversation about how they got to their position. Ask whether they are free for a coffee (or a quick Skype call), or even if they would consider taking you on to do some contracting work on the side while you assess the industry and what the job entails. Many people may be surprised at how successful this approach can be.

- Say yes to everything – including any opportunity that includes meeting new people and getting outside the legal bubble.

- Research professional bodies that relate to an area you're interested in and see what events they host and promote.

- Tell everyone you know that you're interested in moving on and what you might be interested in – and even ask them to let you know if they hear of anything exciting. Your name will come to mind whenever an opportunity arises.

Deanne's Story: "Talk to a variety of people"

In terms of making my decision to move on, the most helpful thing for me was to talk to people – both those that I worked with and all sorts of other people working in a host of other professions. I wanted to know what they thought about their jobs, and whether I was being unrealistic or naïve with my own disappointment.

I wanted to hear all of the arguments as to why I should stick it out. I wanted to be told all of the arguments about why the risk of leaving was too great. I wanted to test my mentality; I didn't want to make a mistake. But none of the arguments were any good – none of them made me think that I was making a mistake. For each one I felt that I had an inarguable counter-argument. Not a counter-argument that could be applied to anyone, because it doesn't work like that. It's entirely subjective.

What matters for me is that I had (and still have) inarguable counter-arguments. I heard everyone else's arguments against leaving, I listened to them, and I understood the reasoning and why it mattered. But after all of that, there was always something in my rationale that made them useless in my case.

This process was phenomenally useful for me. It really helped me to establish mental clarity about the decision to go. If anyone could have given me a good reason to stay, then I would have thought really seriously about it. But there weren't any good reasons.

3. MAKE SENSE

Ibarra suggests learning to reframe past events, along with framing what is happening today, and build a story that links the two together.

A strong story will provide a clearer picture of yourself, which strengthens deep change, updated priorities, and new conceptions of the self. These stories can take time to form.

Ibarra says to give yourself time. You will linger between the old and the new selves, and that is normal. The transition could take three months, or three years – nobody knows. There will be confusion, uncertainty, and turmoil; a loss of routines, peers, and well-rehearsed stories. Stick with the discomfort.

DEANNE'S STORY: "WHERE I AM NOW"

After completing my training contract, I spent six months unemployed and looking for a job (any job) in TV. I was lucky enough to get a place on the BBC's Production Trainee scheme which was a brilliant way into the industry and which launched my career in TV drama. Since then I've spent three and a half years working my way up, on various dramas for the BBC and independent production companies. I'm currently working for Kudos Film and TV.

I am a TV script editor and film producer. I work with the writers, producers and directors to edit the scripts for TV dramas such as Ch4's Utopia and Sky Atlantic's The Tunnel, whilst producing short films in my spare time.

Law is a very well respected thing to have done – people are always impressed by it. The fact I had left such a stable and lucrative career helped demonstrate my passion and commitment to my new chosen industry. Also, my legal background has proved useful for certain elements of producing, which has been a bonus.

I now work in a VERY different environment than I was used to (in a good way) and that did take some adjusting to.

My parents thought I was mad but were always supportive. Friends were split between thinking it was a bold, brave thing to do and thinking I was a bit stupid and it would never work. There will always be detractors but you can't listen to them.

Working in TV was something I'd always had a huge passion for and interest in. But I'd never met anyone who worked in the industry and it felt like a pipe dream. Meeting people who were actually doing it made me realise maybe I could too.

* * *

LEARN, EXPERIMENT, NETWORK

In summary, instead of traveling indefinitely, effective long-term solutions in career transition often involve Learning, Experimenting, and Networking:

– Learning to be really honest with yourself about what actually matters to you;

– Educating yourself on the new career territory you're trying to explore, whether it's through books, events, or courses;

– Reaching out for opportunities to reflect on your blind spots, whether it's with a coach, psychologist, or someone else;

– Building supportive peer networks that help ease the transition; and

– Cultivating new habits by mapping a new blueprint – figuring out your dreams, what it takes to make them into reality, then shaping the parts of the puzzle that you can control into what you envision.

IN A NUTSHELL

» "Exposing yourself to new ideas (learning), new experiences (experimenting) and new people (networking) is the best way of opening yourself up to new possibilities. And you can do ALL of this without quitting your job," explains Escape founder Rob Symington.

» According to Daniel Pink, the three ingredients of fulfilling work are autonomy, mastery, and purpose. Design a series of experiments to help you find that work instead of expecting yourself to know what you cannot know.

» Shifting careers happens when you craft experiments, shift connections, and reframe past events into a new story.

FURTHER RESOURCES

» de Botton, Alain. *The Pleasures and Sorrows of Work.* Vintage, 2010. Print.

» D'Souza, Steven. *Not Knowing: The Art of Turning Uncertainty into Possibility.* LID Publishing Inc, 2014. Print.

» Crane, Ethan. "How Can I Make The Escape From My Career Less Terrifying?" *Escape The City.* 1 Feb 2015. Web. 5 Mar. 2015. <http://www.escapethecity.org/blog/get-unstuck/can-make–escape-career-less-terrifying>

» Esbrand, Janine. "Not Knowing: The Art Of Turning Uncertainty Into Opportunity". *Escape The City.* 1 Dec. 2014. Web. 10 Mar. 2015. <http://www.escapethecity.org/blog/exciting–opportunities/notes–night-knowing-art-turning-uncertainty–opportunity>

» Ibarra, Herminia. *Working Identity: Unconventional Strategies for Reinventing Your Career.* Harvard Business School, 2003. Print.

» Pendry, Jane. "How to Explain the 'Next Steps', When the 'Next Steps' are Unknown." *Escape The City.* 1 Jan. 2015. Web. 4 Mar. 2015. <http://www. escapethecity.org/blog/exciting-opportunities/ explain-next-steps-next–steps-unknown>

» Pink, Daniel. *Drive: The Surprising Truth About What Motivates Us.* Riverhead, 2011. Print.

» Trinetti, Matt. "How Can I Land My Dream Job?" *Escape The City.* 1 Jan. 2015. Web. 7 Mar. 2015. http:// www.escapethecity.org/blog/exciting-opportunities/ how-can-i-land-my-dream-job

EXERCISES

» Identify three areas that interest you and create a profile on Meetup (meetup.com/). Book yourself in for one event in each area, and go along with questions that you are interested in exploring. Also see Eventbrite (eventbrite.co.uk/).

» Design an experiment that would help you to get a better insight into a new area that you might be interested in working in. Create a spreadsheet of potentially helpful people, books, and resources.

HOW I ESCAPED: PETE'S STORY

"If I had stayed in my job, the 'what-if'
thought would have eaten me alive!"

I left the law because I felt that I had to take the leap of faith and go full-time on the start-up I had co-founded. It was becoming impossible to balance both progressing with Mopp (the start-up) and working full-time at DLA Piper and the time felt right (although very risky).

I had been at DLA from joining as a trainee in 2008 until 2013, at which point I was a three year qualified lawyer in the London corporate team. I had been set on the legal career path since accepting DLA's job offer at the end of my second year at the University of Sheffield. It was a great five years. I learned a huge amount from exceptionally talented colleagues, made great friends and was able to work on big ticket deals. However, I had had the start-up urge for a while and once you've started down that track, you can't shake it off.

Mopp is an online platform that allows you to book a trusted cleaner online in 60 seconds. My co-founder and I founded Mopp late in 2012 after repeated terrible experience trying to find a reliable cleaner in London. We both had busy jobs and trying to find a cleaner who was trustworthy and reliable was eating into what little free time we had! The more we researched the industry the more outdated it looked. Domestic cleaning in the UK is a multi-billion pound industry but has shied away from any sort of innovation favouring the cash-in-hand and offline model. We saw a huge opportunity.

Things moved very quickly with Mopp. We worked a lot on the idea over Christmas 2012 and then began the development of a test site. I handed in my notice with DLA two months before we actually launched. It was very risky, but I knew that my three-month notice period would be a big issue if Mopp took off as we thought it would and it could hinder the progress of the business.

My co-founder and I both took the decision that if we were going to leave our careers, we had to go all in on Mopp and not try it part-time with some other work on the side. There are different opinions on this, but I strongly believe that if you want to run a start-up you have to totally commit to it. Nothing can distract from driving the business forwards. Every day counts and if you have to sacrifice two or three days a week for separate work, that is time that your competitors will use to steal a march on you.

After qualifying, I kept getting a feeling that I would want to try something different in the next couple of years, whether it was starting a business or travelling (ironic after a six-year slog to become a qualified lawyer!). I saved a decent amount of my salary every month over three years, which has allowed me to bootstrap Mopp and get by. My lifestyle has completely changed in terms of spending however. I am an expert on Sainsbury's basics range!

I spoke a lot with my Dad who was a great support in listening when I droned on about the pros and cons of staying with DLA or taking the plunge. Tom (my co-founder) and I also talked it through a ton as we were both going to be giving up a lot career-wise to start Mopp.

Ultimately though we knew we had to do it. If I had stayed in my job, the 'what-if' thought would have eaten me alive!

My legal experience has been invaluable (particularly having qualified into the corporate team). Everything from setting up our company, drafting terms and conditions to doing the legals on our first investment round are things which we would have had to pay a good chunk of cash for if neither of us had had legal experience.

Another benefit has been having access to contacts who have added real value e.g. investors, experienced business owners, accountants etc, all whom I met through my time at DLA. One of our seed investors was actually the client on the first corporate deal I led so it has even helped us raise seed capital.

Risk is definitely something that you have to get used to quickly. However, there is a big difference between calculated risk taking and reckless risk taking! I have generally always been quite comfortable with risk (not sure what this says about me as a lawyer....) so haven't found the transition a huge challenge.

One thing that takes more getting used to is the sheer number of decisions that have to be made on a daily basis. This ranges from little things like which accountancy software should you go with through to much bigger decisions like should we spend a significant sum on a new domain and rebrand. It is easy to get into a state of decision paralysis and you quickly get forced into making gut decisions. Some of them may prove to be wrong but the best thing is to make the decision quickly and move fast to correct it if it proves to be wrong. The worst thing is to dawdle and fret about every decision.

One of the best pieces of advice I received when we were starting up was that if you are completely happy with the service/product at the point of launch then you have launched too late.

We are big fans of the lean start-up method and continually use lean principles as we grow. An example of this was the launch of our first website. We were eager to get a test site up as quickly as possible to test whether our idea would resonate with consumers. We therefore had our first site live in three weeks from start to finish. This involved a lot of late nights and weekends (I was still at DLA at the time), but it proved extremely useful in finding out whether our idea had legs early on and not wasting months developing something that could have failed completely.

My family has been as supportive as I could have asked for with no 'but think what you are giving up' questioning (although they may have been thinking it!). Friends have also been supportive but I think a lot of people thought we were slightly loopy to leave City careers to start what they saw as just a cleaning company!

Being completely honest, it takes a little bit of time to get comfortable with being out of the City and not the one with the secure career at a top firm. You have to get any sort of an ego completely in check. This was magnified for me when I bumped into three ex-clients in one day when handing out flyers near St Paul's in July! I won't soon forget the initial looks on their faces when they saw me in a bright blue t-shirt with a big Mopp logo shouting to anyone who would listen about a new cleaning company.

I had always been interested in how businesses operate, but it was during my six months as a corporate trainee that my interest really started. Spending time with entrepreneurs made me want to be on the other side of the table on the deal as the really interesting time starts once the deal is done and the business progresses.

The best advice that I've received is to do things that don't scale. As a start-up, the temptation is to try and act like very big and established companies. Instead, it's more effective to make sure you excel in areas that more established competitors can't compete with.

A great example is customer service. At Mopp, we provide a level of customer service that bigger companies can't match e.g. answering customer queries at 11pm on a Friday evening and personal phone calls to customers from the founders. Although you won't be able to keep doing certain things as you get bigger, it provides a fantastic platform from which to build your brand.

Running a start-up is full of insane highs and lows so you need to develop a tough streak and have the resilience to push on during the tough times as there will be plenty of them. This is the main reason to make sure you have a co-founder. I can't imagine going through this alone!

As we launched Mopp before I left DLA, it was a case of leaving the DLA office for the last time on 19 April 2013 and heading straight to Mopp HQ (our kitchen table at the time!).

Since then, it has been a breakneck journey. We grew rapidly from June 2013 to Christmas 2013 when we raised a £1.3 million seed investment from one of Europe's leading venture capitalist firms.

2014 has also been a great year for us. We went from a turnover of circa £100K and a team of 5 people in January to a £4.5 million (+) turnover and 30-person team by August. In September, we were acquired by Handy.com (the leading online home services marketplace in the US). It has been a breakneck journey without much time off to say the least but hugely fulfilling. The Sunday fear I used to get in my corporate law days is most definitely a thing of the past.

Running Mopp is definitely more time intensive than a legal career (I wasn't sure that was possible before we started...). An average week for me at the moment will be about 90 hours, working every day. However, I have much more flexibility in organising my day now, which makes a huge difference. I feel much more in control of my life. Working for yourself is a hell of a lot more rewarding than putting all your effort into creating value for someone else's company.

The benefits far outweigh the drawbacks but you have to start a business with your eyes open. The main issue is the loss of financial security for an extended period of time. Only after seven months in with Mopp did we take a salary. Holidays, new clothes and meals out go out the window!

In terms of inspiration, from a personal point of view, Stephen Wall at Pho was a big inspiration. I was part of the DLA team that acted for Pho on their equity investment and got to know Stephen well. He left a career in marketing to travel the world and then set up what has become a multimillion pound restaurant brand with his wife Jules. Hi story was definitely an influence on me taking the start-up plunge with Mopp. Another ex-client, Mark Beilby at Lumi Mobile, who founded a start-up after 24 years as one of the top TMT analysts in the City, has also been a great support.

Ryan Graves at Uber is another person I look up to. I've never met him but his rise from a career at GE to Global Head of Operations at Uber takes some beating. They are a great company and I love the culture they have developed within their business. Results-driven, work seriously hard but enjoy yourself. That's what it is about.

* * *

[6]

PREPARING
FINANCIALLY

*"Money is like gasoline during a road trip. You
don't want to run out of gas on your trip, but
you're not doing a tour of gas stations."*

–Tim O'Reilly

"He's so much happier," a friend told me over lunch,
speaking about her partner who had recently left his job
in order to explore starting his own business. "He's more
present, he's more attentive, and it's definitely the right
thing for him…"

She trailed off and I could sense that there was a 'but'
coming. Sure enough, after a couple of silent moments, she
sighed.

"What?" I nudged.

"Until we go to a dinner party!" she said. "It's so hard
when we're meeting people we don't know. They ask him
what he's doing now and it becomes obvious that I'm the
one supporting both of us at the moment. He gets so quiet
and weird on the way home."

I nodded, as I'd seen this with numerous Escape members, who felt comfortable with their decision to leave until they had to start explaining it to other people.

Then the questions would start – *how are you going to pay your mortgage or rent? How are you going to survive day-to-day? Are you worried about the long-term salary hit?* And then the really uncomfortable questions that didn't get asked, would linger unspoken – *aren't you scared that you won't be able to afford what the rest of us are working so hard to provide?*

Money is about more than salary and mortgages – it is about power, control, and freedom. Your financial position is linked to your family's financial position. Your attitudes towards money are often influenced by your parents and peers. Your opinion on money is unique and expecting everyone to share your view is naïve.

For that reason, I cannot tell you how to deal with your finances or cater to everyone's individual concerns with money. For the same reason, you will not be able to control how friends, family and strangers respond to your financial choices. Still, this chapter gives you some ideas on what other people have done to deal with the money situation when considering an escape from the legal profession.

Financial position is obviously a major concern for most people looking to leave the law. This is hardly surprising, given what we have explored to date in relation to lawyers' pessimism bias as well as a tendency towards creating a surefire plan *before* jumping off the ledge. Also, it would be hard not to get accustomed to the lifestyle of being a well-paid lawyer.

I have never had to step away from the salary of a City law firm in order to pursue my dreams. I dropped out of law school as a fairly cash-strapped 22-year-old student and became a little less-cash-strapped 22-year-old freelancer. I'm aware that I am not in a position to advise on the money question when it comes to transitioning away from City lawyer salaries. So instead, I wanted to point out some helpful approaches to dealing with the money question.

First of all, it's important to acknowledge that money is an emotional issue. Our relationship with money often reveals some of our deepest fears and insecurities. This is a point beautifully illustrated in a *New York Times* op-ed ('For the Love of Money') written by former hedge-fund trader Sam Polk:

"In my last year on Wall Street my bonus was $3.6 million — and I was angry because it wasn't big enough," he said. He talked openly about overcoming his wealth addiction, and about how with the help of a counselor, he started to see he was living his life based on fear.

"I was accumulating money so I could pretend I was protected," he said. "Instead, I saw I should live a life based on adventure and expressing myself in the world."

While your own internal debate might not be based upon the same numbers as Polk, you might be approaching the money question from a similar set of fears. Money is a legitimate way of protecting ourselves against life's curveballs. The amount that we need and the price we are willing to pay for it is entirely up to us.

Katherine, who as previously mentioned helped to edit this book, made the transition from a stable, well-paying job as a lawyer to a less financially secure position involving a mix of travelling, volunteering and paid contracting work.

She points out that a certain amount of money is essential for basic obligations and daily living costs. Not everyone can up and move to a country that has a low cost of living while they develop their startup, or stay in London but cut all of their living expenses overnight.

"With that in mind, obviously it is worth mentioning that there is a fundamental need to save, build an escape fund as much as possible and reduce expenses if you are planning to leave the law. However, beyond making this initial point I think it is patronising to offer advice on how to structure weekly budgets, or that 'cutting out a daily latte could result in a savings of £2,000 a year!'"

When it comes to specific advice like this, it would be almost impossible to cater to the individual lifestyle and earning circumstances of a very broad range of people who might be turning to this book for guidance. This kind of advice, I believe, also fails to get to the heart of the concerns many escapees have when considering leaving the law.

"Focusing on the small picture – that is, the day-to-day issues of budgeting, spending patterns and cutting back on luxuries – may be a useful strategy for the short term, while you're building your escape fund and planning a new direction. Yet there is also a case for taking a big picture view of your finances and your income and embracing a new, creative, approach to money that could help you to take the plunge and finally move away from the security of a lawyer's salary."

Katherine believes that a useful first step is to acknowledge that you're leaving a stable income and potentially taking a risk. However, embracing the risk you're taking is important. If you want to leave law, it is likely because you acknowledge that it does not serve your best interests and it doesn't fulfill you in the way that another career path or venture might. Although you may be leaving behind a good salary, taking this risk will ultimately allow you to make a move that could be more rewarding, inspiring and fulfilling.

This approach also helps with reconceptualising your pre-existing salary. How much is it costing you, to earn that generous wage? While you may be getting paid well, that salary may represent dissatisfaction, unhappiness, poor health and contribute to unfulfilling relationships, as well as professional dissatisfaction. Leaving it all behind is very likely to be an investment in your long-term happiness.

It can be hard to change your thinking like this, Katherine says:

"When you're working long hours in a law firm and then spending much of your free time with friends in professional services, it is natural to internalise the values of this environment. Within this world, it is the unspoken but pervasive and predominant opinion that success is defined by your status within the law firm and the salary that you earn. It can also be hard to step outside of this bubble to see how other people are earning a living or what other options are out there for you."

It is easy to buy into this world when your day-to-day life and all the people in it value and prioritise this way of living. However, this model and these priorities are not the only ones – expanding your circles and meeting other people will help you realise this.

Leaving the law and making it work, financially, may require self-confidence, resourcefulness and a creative mindset. Katherine talks about how it was useful to tap into the confidence of her more entrepreneurial friends when making the decision to leave her lawyer's salary behind. By talking to friends who were pursuing start up ideas or working in creative industries, she realised that necessity often breeds inventive ways of overcoming roadblocks. She tried to channel their optimism about the future and their confidence that they were resourceful enough to just make it work.

Katherine's ideas align with the approach that Sam took to the money question, as he explains below.

SAM'S STORY (CONT'D): "THE LIMITATIONS OF MONEY AS A JUSTIFICATION"

I often thought (and still do think) that for every success story that I'm looking to emulate, there are so many people who completely bombed. For every famous footballer, you have a load of kids who sacrificed a lot and gave everything to become a professional player but didn't make it. The same goes for actors: for every Oscar winner, there are a huge host of pretenders waiting tables. And people often used that as an argument in support of making 'sensible' decisions: "sure, we all want this dream career, but how many people really get it?"

My mentality is very much that if I don't take the risk and put myself out there, I certainly won't achieve anything. I know that I will never be happy doing what I was doing. So I feel that I should just take a shot at being happy, and if it doesn't work I'll go and do something else. You have to back yourself.

I think I'm lucky that I have a lot of self-confidence, I'm very willing to take risks, and I don't worry too much about what

---

might happen. Maybe it's a bit irresponsible, but what it comes down to is that I'd sooner be irresponsible and happy then responsible and miserable.

The money thing is unquestionably an issue for me. I haven't always lived frugally and ideally I wouldn't have to. I don't like the financial insecurity that I've brought on myself, but I'm able to justify that when balanced with the other things that I want out of life.

Ultimately, I would love to have loads of money because I would love the freedom that I think that would give me. But the type of money that I'd get from working in law or a similar corporate job is far from being the huge, huge money that I can really get excited about. I want the type of money you get from setting up your own business and selling it as a huge success. I want retire-at-35 money. And if I can't have that – then I'd rather do something that I'm passionate about and that makes me happy, than do something I hate for mid-level money.

"But what about your kids? How are you going to pay their school fees?" That's what people always say to me. I've got absolutely no idea, but in my mind that kind of question doesn't come close to impacting my decision as to what to do professionally at this stage of my life. If I live a life stifled by that kind of logic at every turn, then how many opportunities am I going to miss out on, before I even have kids?

Maybe I'm irresponsible and maybe I should think about the future more, but if I did think like that then maybe I wouldn't be doing what I'm doing now. And if I wasn't, I know for certain that I'd still be unhappy. Having made the leap I feel completely re-energised and am inspired and motivated to achieve again. Plus I'm having so much fun. So I can't worry about money too much, and certainly not about mid-level money.

Since my job offered no desirable goal in terms of the work that I would be doing later down the line, was continuing along that road justifiable on the grounds of money? Is professional discontentment sufficiently saved by a plump pay-cheque? At this point, my sixteen-year-old self would be doing up his tie and reaching for his cufflinks, but sixteen is sixteen and misery is a real revelation.

It's all a balancing act, and I would gladly take that money for that job if I only had to work for two hours a day, but I wouldn't if I had to work for twelve hours, let alone twenty. Seth Godin said it: "Many people are starting to realise that they work a lot and that working on stuff they believe in (and making things happen) is much more satisfying than just getting a pay cheque and waiting to get fired (or die)."

I knew that money couldn't justify that job for me.

The biggest thing for me was that, if I were to continue on that path, I would be showing a monumental lack of aspiration relative to my values. I couldn't reconcile this with how I had lived my life up until that point. I couldn't reconcile it with the view that I had of myself (rightly or wrongly).

The culture that I experienced at work felt out-dated, inefficient and inexplicably and unjustifiably hierarchical. In short, it was entirely removed from the real world, where interaction, discussion and questioning were natural, and productive. The real world, where other people enjoyed work and where I enjoyed my life. I wanted stimulation, invigoration, and to work with progressive people with progressive attitudes doing things that I really, passionately, gave a shit about.

I was living an uninspiring, non-committal life characterised by apathy, boredom, a lack of direction and an unnerving desire to not be doing what I was doing. It's hardly the cocktail of happiness, is it? Quite clearly, any benefit I could draw from my predicament wasn't worth the unhappiness that I was feeling. Not with this job, not with this compensation, not with this dearth of fulfillment

* * *

USING YOUR LEGAL SKILLS TO ESCAPE

As we've discussed above, reconceptulising your salary and adopting an inner confidence and a creative outlook can help when dealing with the "money issue" that inevitably arises when planning or making your escape from the law. Although there are many creative ways to ensure some financial stability while exploring a move away from law, it is true that many lawyers tap into their skills and expertise as lawyers when planning, or implementing their escape from the law.

The stories in this chapter will give you an insight into how your legal skills and background could be put to good use while planning your escape, and importantly, growing your escape fund.

I've talked to many lawyers who have done just this and it has become clear that it is a popular option to work flexibly as a lawyer or legal assistant on a contracting or freelancing basis. Although this concept can be manifested in many different ways, I have noticed that there are three popular ways to make a freelance legal career work while considering an escape from the law. The first is to approach your employer and negotiate flexible hours. Secondly, many lawyers I have spoken with have found work as freelancers with one of the many emerging freelance lawyer firms or networks. Finally, and particularly in London, high volume legal process outsourcing work has become popular as an option for lawyers considering an escape.

These options will be explored in further detail below.

DANIEL'S STORY: "NEGOTIATING FLEXIBLE HOURS"

Daniel van Binsbergen is now the CEO and cofounder of Lexoo, an online legal marketplace connecting businesses to specialised lawyers. Lexoo raised $1.3 million in funding in November 2015. Daniel's entrepreneurial journey began when he stayed on at his firm but as a flexible associate instead of a full-time employee.

I couldn't picture myself essentially doing the same job until retirement and I also felt that my learning curve started to flatten out. As I was always interested in entrepreneurship I started to spend a lot of time reading books and blogs about start-ups. As a result, I became more familiar with that path and I could picture myself trying that. Then it was just a question of picking a date to hand in my notice, save as much as I could in the meantime, and come up with some sort of plan and business idea and going for it!

Even as a junior lawyer you earn quite a bit more than some of your peers, plus every year you get a raise. So I decided early on that my junior lawyer salary should be sufficient for the next couple of years. My idea was that whenever I would get a raise, I would just increase the standing order to my savings account by the same amount. So over the years I never gave myself more spending money than I had as a junior lawyer, but the amount I was able to save monthly would increase significantly every year. This had the added benefit of not getting used to a very expensive lifestyle, which made adjusting to start-up life after I quit all the easier.

When I submitted my notice the firm asked me to reconsider and indicated they would love to keep me on board. I then indicated I would also appreciate not severing ties completely, and suggested I continue to work for them on an ad hoc/contractor basis. The firm was fine with this, and so I was able to continue to work on some small files, usually from home. I should mention that I had these discussions with HR/management, and not with the partners I used to work for. It worked out quite well in that I was able to work an average of two and a half hours a day for about six months after I quit, which gave me time to try out different ideas (I worked on two other ideas before launching lexoo.co.uk).

The firm was much more flexible than I had expected. So you might be surprised what is possible if you ask. Also, more and more firms like to have a flexible pool of ex-associates (also from other firms) that they can hire on a freelance basis as and when they need it, for instance for an unexpected amount of due diligence work. My old firm is now formalising such a flexible pool as well, although it didn't yet exist when I quit. If you have a bit of your own client following you could also consider starting out for yourself or join a virtual firm that does all the admin/ insurance for you, in exchange for (usually around) 30% of your fees. This would also give you way more time during the day to work on your own business.

When I told my direct boss (a partner) that I was going to quit, I believe he mentioned this to a member of the firm's board after I told him. I'm guessing that he probably indicated that it would be worth trying to get me to stay on.

I then received a phone call from the board member who asked me to reconsider. I indicated that I would be very much interested in thinking up a way that I could stay involved with the firm in a more flexible way but not on an employment basis. I sent him an e-mail pitching my idea of being a contractor for them. He replied that this was something the firm was already looking at more generally (to create a flexible layer), so that he was fine with it.

I contacted HR to discuss the specifics. After the freelance contract was in place I told the partners I used to work for I could continue to work on matters as a flexible associate.

Daniel's story shows how lawyers can have the opportunity to redefine their role with their pre-existing employer – from full time employee to contractor.

However, there are many different versions of contracting that are available to lawyers who might want to use their existing legal skills (and perhaps don't have the option of contracting to their former firm). There has been a recent trend within the legal industry to embrace and develop alternative ways of providing legal services and therefore alternative ways of engaging lawyers. Lawyers seeking to use their legal skills while planning or implementing an escape from the law are fortunate to have a range of options available to them in this new climate.

* * *

FLEXIBLE LEGAL RESOURCING

One option available is to engage as a freelance lawyer with one of the many emerging firms that are best described as flexible legal resourcing businesses.

Although each of these firms differ in their structure, business plan and methodology, lawyers generally work as contractors for these businesses and are engaged to do on site, or remote work for clients and law firms, on an "as needed" basis.

London-based businesses such as Lawyers on Demand, Keystone Law, Obelisk and Axiom are gaining traction and steadily increasing the number of freelance lawyers on their books, as well as the number of clients requiring a more flexible approach to legal services.

As is mentioned on the Lawyers on Demand website, these businesses are "designed for talented lawyers who want to work differently". With greater autonomy and control over their working week, freelance lawyers can use this model to spend more time developing their own business, travelling or even re-training.

As Daniel's story mentioned, other business models of this nature are linked to law firms. Some examples are Allen and Overy's Peerpoint business, Freshfield's Continuum, Pinsent Masons' Vario and Eversheds' Agile.

As the legal industry continues to expand, evolve and explore new ways of providing services to clients, so to do the opportunities available to lawyers who may be wishing to work more independently. Such independence and flexibility can only be useful as an additional option for those lawyers who are saving in order to leave the law.

LEGAL PROJECT CONTRACTING

Another version of legal contracting which has proven popular recently has been to work for large firms on a specific project or transaction. In this context, which has been described as "legal process outsourcing" or "project contracting", a large number of lawyers are engaged to do the "behind-the-scenes" work on a specific stage of a transaction, such as due diligence or discovery.

During this transaction, the project contractors typically will have the option to work full time hours (or even overtime) but have flexibility around the workload they take on. It is this flexibility, and the generous hourly pay rates that have attracted many lawyers to project contracting as a means to travel, develop business ideas, do further study and, most importantly, save money.

While project contracting may not be a long-term option due to the minimal progression opportunities it offers, and though the work can be repetitive, it offers a well-paying alternative to unemployment.

Escape members doing project contracting work in London share below.

WHAT KIND OF WORK IS OUT THERE?
"Most of the work is due diligence, discovery or regulatory investigation. In my role assisting with a regulatory investigation, the day-to-day work is to use online databases to search for certain types of content and to code each individual document (either as responsive or not responsive and then with the relevant tags and categories of content). Responsive content is then forwarded to a second level reviewer to be checked and collated and then eventually onto the lawyers on the project."

WHAT'S THE PAY LIKE?
"The money varies, but pay is by the hour. The pay can vary a lot – between about £15 – £40 an hour as the base

rate. The main difference comes down to whether or not overtime is available on the particular project."

"Overtime on week nights is billed at a rate of time and a half (usually with a maximum of 12 total hours working in a day) and in the weekend, it can be double time. So if you can get on a project with a lot of overtime available, you can work long hours and make a decent amount of cash in a short space of time."

"We are currently only doing eight-hour days but last year we have had full overtime available, so I was billing 12 hours a day, plus weekends. The rates are around £32.00 per hour for the first eight hours, £49.00 for weekday overtime and £65.00 per hour for weekend work. So it stacks up quite quickly. Plus you have absolute freedom over your hours and holidays. So it's flexible and well paid."

HOW HARD IS IT TO GET ROLES?
"If you are qualified as a lawyer in a Commonwealth country, it is relatively easy to find roles. Generally, it is more difficult to obtain a higher paying role and it can be a huge advantage to have a top-tier firm on your resume. At the end of the day though, a lot comes down to luck and individual timing to land a job at the start of a project as availability of work can vary hugely depending on the time of year and the market."

HOW DO YOU GET STARTED?
"The only way to get into contracting work is through recruiters. When registering with a recruiting agency, you will be required to supply supporting documentation for your legal qualifications as well as requested personal information such as your passport and CV. Once registered, you will be contacted when work is available. The client

(whether it be a law firm or an outsourcing firm who is working for a law firm) will contact the recruitment agency and let them know that they need a certain amount of people for a project. The recruiter will then contact you. There is usually a fast turn around time between when you hear from the recruiter and when they need you to start the project – sometimes even the same day."

WHAT IS IT LIKE ON A DAY-TO-DAY BASIS?

"Mostly the work is very mundane, though work as a second-level reviewer can be more varied and interesting, sometimes involving working with the lawyers on the particular case."

"Generally people only choose to work as a document reviewer to make some quick cash while they search for other work and these roles provide great flexibility to apply for jobs, attend interviews or develop alternative career ideas. I know a lot of people who take contracting roles while doing further study, or working on entrepreneurial projects and start ups. Having this mental stimulation on the side can help counteract the repetitive work that contracting often involves."

"Sometimes projects can run for months and it can be a great lifestyle, with low stress, good pay and flexible hours."

MARK'S STORY: "DOCUMENT REVIEW"

For many years the preserve of foreign-qualified lawyers, and dominated by Antipodeans, more and more UK-qualified lawyers are becoming aware of the highly lucrative document review

---

contractor industry and the flexibility and freedom it gives to people who don't want to follow the traditional law firm or in-house career track.

Document review lawyers are brought it to assist on large scale disclosure exercises on behalf of large City law firms and, occasionally, legal outsourcing companies. Lawyers are generally engaged by a recruitment agency and paid by them. Hourly salaries range from £18-25 per hour for paralegal type roles and go up to £30-50 per hour for better roles at larger firms such as Slaughter and May, Clifford Chance and Hogan Lovells. Firms generally pay overtime once you have completed eight hours, starting at time and a half and sometimes increasing to double time after 11-12 hours or for weekend work. This means you can earn some serious money.

Many contractors structure their payments through a traditional limited company or, alternatively, an umbrella company through organisations such as Network One (reputably very popular with contractors) or Danbro. Umbrella companies offer a hybrid arrangement where you are employed by a separate company and given shares in it to enable you to take income as dividends as well as being able to utilise capital gain tax allowances (I know, it sounds complex). These offer significant tax advantages and can allow contractors to take home in excess of 80% of what they earn – versus around 60-65% for PAYE employees. You also will earn a higher hourly rate, as the agency shares the national insurance contribution savings with you. Obviously there are risks associated with this and I would advise you to take some form of tax advice before committing to using either of these structures.

The work itself is pretty mundane, involving reviewing hundreds of documents each day for particular keywords and relevance to the wider case. Work is often split into tier 1 and tier 2 reviews.

Tier 1 normally involves a bog-standard review of all initial documents: relevant and irrelevant. Tier 2 reviews can be more complex, including reviewing the work of more junior reviewers and/or liaising with Counsel and drafting documents such as witness statements or pleadings. Tier 2 is generally considered to be more interesting work but it really depends what you are after – some people enjoy the mindless clicking of tier 1 reviews and the ability to just come in, bash out eight hours work, and go home.

In recent years, quite a lot of the projects have been in relation to post-recession banking litigation. Projects generally run for several months but being contentious, can end at any time (and your engagement with it: contracts are normally zero notice). Some firms bring document reviewers in for smaller projects and these can last from a few days to several weeks. If you impress on a project, you can sometimes be moved from one project to another and I've heard of some contractors remaining at a firm for two or three years. However, this kind of goes against what I see as the biggest advantage of document review: freedom. You are generally expected to work eight hours per day but, in reality, there is a large degree of flexibility. If you take time off, you don't earn any money (holiday is usually incorporated into the hourly rate). I've heard of some contractors revolving between working three months, then taking three months off, then working three months and so on. In the current market, projects seem to be quite easy to come by for those with a decent City pedigree and demonstrable disclosure experience. I relied on experience gained as a trainee working on large scale disclosure exercises on several discrimination cases, so certainly not banking litigation related.

Due to the nature of some of the cases, the risk of conflicts arising is quite high. This means that fresh meat can sometimes be preferred to experienced document reviewers. Anecdotally, some firms will not use the some document reviewer more than once.

Some roles require you to have a practising certificate – this can be purchased on an individual basis by calling the SRA and costs around £300 for one year, and decreases in price throughout the year (as practising certificates run from October to September). Job titles vary from paralegal to contract lawyer but all involve pretty much the same work. I understand that, technically, if you are a qualified solicitor, you should remove yourself from the solicitor's roll before embarking on a role as a paralegal, but in practice many firms don't seem to care.

The working environment can vary greatly from firm to firm. The document review community is quite transient and people are always leaving or joining. This means that at a lot of places you won't be greeted by the team or given an office tour, just shown a computer and given the particulars of claim. This can be hard to adapt to if you've previously worked in a close-knit environment and is something to bear in mind before accepting a position (many of which involve absolutely no interview process – just sending your CV via an agent!).

A final word of warning, before embarking on a career in document review (and/or including it on your CV) you should be aware that it is not viewed particularly highly in relation to permanent positions, in either a private practice or in-house context. In some cases, it can be detrimental to your application and you shouldn't start document review work thinking that you can easily return to a "regular" legal position. By the very nature of the work (repetitive, low level and not intellectually challenging), it does not give you a huge amount of ammunition to discuss in an interview situation. However, if you're after some serious cash (easily £100k+ if you can get some overtime on a rate of £35 or thereabouts, with or without the added benefits of the tax structuring outlined above) and don't care about a legal "career" in the traditional sense, then I highly recommend *exploring this interesting area of City law. The reality is, if after a couple of days you completely hate it, you leave!*

Whilst personal experience differs, a couple of good agencies that I have worked with or had recommended to me include Michael Page, BCL Legal, Law Absolute, City Law Solutions, Consolio (a big legal outsourcing company) and Ryder Reid.

* * *

KATIE'S STORY: "I THINK ABOUT WHAT I AM MOVING TOWARDS"

I remember my perspective being changed forever when I used to talk about my future with a good friend. He simply could not understand that I was scared to leave my job because I therefore wouldn't have any money. He was a very entrepreneurial, resourceful and confident person and he just knew that he would be okay and would get by without a stable income because he would just simply have to make it work. Therefore, it would work.

He just didn't relate to my risk adverse tendencies and would have a comeback for every barrier I raised with him. He pointed out that, as a trained lawyer with many years experience at a well-respected firm, I have marketable skills, I have contacts and, ultimately, I work hard. He used to say that there was just no way that I would ever be left sleeping under a bridge.

I remember nodding along, but deep down being baffled about his approach, still thinking, "Well, yes, that's all well and good, but how do I pay the rent?"

That was a couple of years ago and now that I think about it, my approach has certainly changed. I've left the big law firm and, it is true, I don't sleep under a bridge. I've let go of thinking that a stable income is the only way I can make money and have been forced to expand my perspective toward other ways of earning an income, putting my skills to good use and marketing myself. Since I left the law, I've done a mixture of travelling, consulting, legal contracting work and volunteer work while planning my next steps. Now that I'm outside the legal industry's bubble, I do buy into my friend's way of thinking a lot more and I feel confident that things will be okay and that the lawyer's pay cheque is not an essential requirement in my life.

There are many ways to make money that don't involve working in a law firm that doesn't inspire or challenge you. The reality is that many former lawyers have managed to create a new life for themselves that does work, like Jodi Ettenberg, a former lawyer who is particularly inspiring and open about her move away from the law. Jodi founded the popular travel/food blog called 'Legal Nomads' (legalnomads.com/) and has written before about how she has managed to leave behind a well-paying legal job to travel and, eventually, create her own income by drawing on her marketable skills. Now, she travels the world and earns a living through social media consulting work, selling merchandise and products through her site, food tours, freelance writing and brand partnerships.

Whenever I talk to friends about their anxieties stemming from leaving the law and therefore their legal income behind, I mention Jodi. Jodi saved hard, left the law to travel and then used her skills to establish her own brand, combining her marketable skills and her interests. Although Jodi took all the right steps in preparation – building her escape fund and budgeting carefully – I imagine that when she decided to quit her job as a lawyer, she thought more about what she was moving towards, that is, the independence and excitement of travelling the world, as opposed to the stable legal salary that she was moving away from.

I try to take this approach whenever I have money anxieties of my own – I think about what I am moving towards and why this is important to me. I trust that I am going to be able to make it work.

* * *

PORTFOLIO INCOMES

Financial position is often a primary concern when considering an escape from the legal profession. Whether it's saving really hard in your current job before resigning; negotiating flexible hours; signing up for contracting work; or constructing an alternative arrangement where your legal skills can be put to use, what works best for you often comes down to your own personal circumstances and preferences.

Speaking to Escape members Susanne and Hannah also reminded me that following interests and building income around those interests is a key characteristic of constructing a protean (or "portfolio") career – the fluid nature of which is a characteristic of career construction in the 21st century (as we explored in the opening chapter):

SUSANNE'S STORY: "LAW AND PSYCHOLOGY"

I have built a portfolio career: I am a trainee lawyer in Berlin, Germany, and a trainee mediator. I am also a lecturer for Law in International Development at the university. In addition, I work as an author in the area of organisational psychology and have just co-authored a book on working with virtual teams. In that context, I have started to consult with international organisations on working with virtual teams.

I got my LLM at the University of London and am training in Berlin, Germany.

For many years, I knew that I didn't want to pursue my legal training, but for a number of reasons (society and family related), I wasn't able to let go of the internal pressure to finish my legal education. In Germany, five years of law school are succeeded by an additional two years of training before admission to the bar.

Even though I had gone down a different path (I had worked for the United Nations for a few years and started to pursue my great passion – psychology – by getting a postgraduate degree at the London School of Economics), I was always afraid that my CV would appear incomplete without the bar admission.

The training is what I expected. It is predominantly formalistic. My current classmates are an interesting mix that reflects how much German society is changing. There are a number that are in their mid thirties and with a lot of international work experience. Most of my classmates with such backgrounds decided to train out of the same fear I have described. The majority of them, however, are in their mid to late twenties.

Some of them are full of doubt about whether this is the right path for them; others seem to be very set on becoming lawyers.

I am thinking of switching out of the law as my interest and talents are not reflected by legal work. Mediation is an exception as it lies at the nexus of law and psychology and I am building a profile there.

I know many lawyers who seem to really enjoy what they do, and I know many who seem to hate it. I believe it comes down to why someone chooses to join the legal profession. If their reasons are authentic and not entirely driven by status and family expectations, law can be as enjoyable as any other profession. But when the heart isn't in it, it becomes hell.

* * *

HANNAH'S STORY: "LAW AND ENTREPRENEURSHIP"

Hannah is currently working part-time as a solicitor, doing private client work and still running This Is Your Kingdom. (thisisyourkingdom.co.uk). She did a law degree at Cardiff University and then trained at CMS Cameron McKenna.

I got a law degree because I thought it was a good degree to get. It wasn't because of any massive desire to be a lawyer.

I think there was a quite a big divide among classmates. There were a lot of people doing it for the academic challenge, who wanted to be a lawyer. Other people were doing it because they liked the idea of being a lawyer but weren't massively aware of what was involved.

I left CMS Cameron McKenna and took voluntary redundancy to take up This Is Your Kingdom. Then I spent a year and a half setting it up and getting it going and then actually found a job with a smaller firm, part-time. Having that balance is what really suits me. I enjoy the legal side of being a lawyer as well as having the time to put into a passion project – the balance of both is what makes me feel most fulfilled.

When you train to be a lawyer or you imagine yourself being a lawyer, you never think that this could be an option. But these days, people are a lot more open to flexi-working or doing other stuff; it's become a lot more normal.

Of course, this isn't the same at magic circle firms. In those environments, it seems to be all or nothing. When you work in a big corporate firm, you work on one big deal and you work on it all hours. There's not that flexibility like there is when you're running your own business. The clients are more demanding and need you there 24/7.

I was really lucky and had a good experience of working at a corporate law firm. The hours were manageable – if you were needed or asked to stay, you had to be there. But there was never pressure to stay late. There was lots of support, lots of great training.

I do like the academic side of law – I enjoy the fact that I have two sides to my career. Running my own business and then doing law use completely different skill-sets but each of them makes me enjoy the other more. I just don't know if I could do one without the other.

* * *

IN A NUTSHELL

» Lifestyles and earning circumstances can differ dramatically between individuals, making it difficult to offer a "one-size-fits-all" approach to the money issue that faces lawyers considering an escape from the law.

» What can often shift during career change is your relationship to money itself.

» Often, lawyers used their existing skills to remain with one foot in the legal profession while pursuing alternative options, or investigating their next step. One option is to change your employment status at your current firm and become a freelance associate or contractor.

FURTHER RESOURCES

» Berman, Casey. "The First Step in Leaving Law Behind – It's the Money, Stupid." *Above the Law.* 18 Jan. 2013. Web. 10 Jan. 2015 <http://abovethelaw.com/career-files/the-first-step-in-leaving-law-behind-its-the-money-stupid/>

» Escape the City. "The Money Question." *The Escape Manifesto: Quit Your Corporate Job – Do Something Different!* Capstone, 2013. Print.

» Shin, Laura. "How Sam Polk, Former Wall Street Trader And 'Wealth Addict,' Broke Free Of His Golden Handcuffs". *Forbes.* 2 Mar. 2014. Web. 14 Feb. 2015. <http://www.forbes.com/sites/laurashin/2014/02/03/how-sam-polk-former-wall-street-trader-and-wealth-addict-broke-free-of-his-golden-handcuffs/>

EXERCISES

» Kate Northrup is a financial coach who offers a free quiz that reveals more about your relationship with money. Visit her site and take the quiz (katenorthrup.com).

» Create a profile and begin to use free financial software to better track your income and expenditure (e.g. Mint in the USA, Money Dashboard in the UK).

HOW I ESCAPED: AMBER'S STORY

"I wanted more out of life than just a title."

I practiced law for ten years. I did the job well and received great reviews. But I always knew I was an outsider. I often wondered what would become of me if I were *too* good at my job.

The partners around me seemed happy enough with their big houses, nice cars, and fancy suits.

They had money to burn. From where I was sitting, though, they were stretched too thin and overworked, many of them divorced, and aging much too quickly. I was forced to decide whether this is what I wanted for my life. The thought of sitting in that office for another 25 or 30 years was overwhelming.

Some people dream of this life. The money and the title are enough for them. But I never dreamed of being a lawyer, let alone a lawyer that helped large corporations pay less tax. And although the money and the title were nice, they never defined me as a person. I wanted more from life.

So I tried to figure out what I *'actually'* enjoy doing – I enjoy spending time with my husband, eating great food, and experiencing new things.

Working at a big law firm just didn't fit the bill. I needed an out and, with a bit of courage, I found one.

I had reached the apex of my career. I was waiting to hear whether I would make partner at the largest law firm in the world. On some days, I thought that was what I wanted. Isn't that what every big law attorney wants?

And then it happened. I heard through the grapevine that I would make partner on July 1, in just over 30 days. This was a big deal, a huge accomplishment. I was working for the largest law firm in the world. The trouble is, I had already decided that I didn't want this life. I was a short timer, and I knew that I would not stay long after making partner. This news threw me into a frenzy of worry. The knot in my stomach just kept growing. I felt sick.

I knew that my boss had vouched for me in the partnership process, that he respected and trusted me. I worried endlessly about what he would think if I quit shortly after I made partner. What would the other partners think? What would my colleagues think? Don't get me wrong: I wanted to escape, but I didn't want to destroy relationships that I valued.

I arrived at my apartment that evening and shared my thoughts and feelings with Eric, my husband. We talked about my "great" news, and he helped me to be certain that our life was on a different path, a better path for us. As I said before, I was a short timer.

I suppose I just hadn't fully appreciated how quickly the time to move on would come. It was then that I decided I would quit the next day. I waltzed in the next morning and told my boss that I was leaving the firm.

After a brief moment of silence, he said, "What will you do? What are your plans?" I told him that I planned to travel and ultimately settle somewhere in Asia, where I would teach yoga or maybe English or sell beers on a beach.

Truth is, I didn't really know exactly what I would do. For once in life, it felt surprisingly great not to have a plan. In the end, he appreciated that I told him when I did. He admired that I had the courage to go in search of a fulfilling life that makes me truly happy. I thanked him for not yelling at me.

Six weeks later, it was over. On my last Friday afternoon at the firm, I stood at the threshold of my office, where I had spent so many years, so many hours endlessly working, and smiled. I knew the next steps would be tough. I knew that not having a plan would be tough. But I felt lighter. One week later, Eric and I were on a plane embarking on a new adventure

You may be wondering why it took me ten years to figure out that I was unhappy. It didn't. I was waiting for partnership – I wanted to "retire" from my career as a partner. I wanted to know that I could accomplish it. But in the end, none of this mattered. I knew I had made it. The position was mine for the taking. I wanted more out of life than just a title. I escaped.

* * *

[7]

EMBRACING
RENEWAL

"I don't believe people are looking for the meaning of life as much as they are looking for the experience of being alive."

–Joseph Campbell

I was in my living room with a friend who openly hated her job as a solicitor. We had been talking about how maybe, if she hated life that much, she should consider looking at other career paths.

I had mentioned this very research and talked about some of the ex-lawyers I'd been interviewing, hinting that plenty of people left the legal profession every day.

"That's great," she kept saying. But her tone made it very clear that career change was an impractical option for her.

Before you can create change in your life, you need to accept the fears that accompany change. These are the same fears that can stop you from even entering into a conversation about how things may be different. These demons can be tough to face and, as we've seen, this is where a coach can come in helpful – helping to lift the fog that can come with self-sabotage and self-doubt.

With or without a coach, before you can map an escape route, it helps to be aware of the broader context that shapes the mapping exercise itself.

My friend had been trained to avoid failure. By ignoring the reality that she didn't enjoy the direction her career was headed in, she could ignore feeling like she had failed when it came to crafting a meaningful professional identity.

SWITCHING MINDSETS

I interviewed Dr Tara Swart, CEO of the Unlimited Mind, Faculty at MIT Sloan and lead author of the book *Neuroscience for Leadership: Harnessing the Brain Gain Advantage*. She referenced Dr Carol Dweck's work on fixed mindsets and growth mindsets.

THE FIXED MINDSET
According to Dweck, a Type 1 or fixed mindset is one that is fearful of making mistakes. All lawyers I've met have embraced this mindset, and if you're reading this, I'm tempted to believe that you're probably of that mindset too: excellent at playing by the rules, great at behaving yourself and a consistent achiever when it comes to good grades, which have led to good degrees and good jobs. You've been indoctrinated to believe that the fixed mindset is the route to success.

You can probably relate to having been trained not to make mistakes – ever. You risk being sacked if you get sloppy with daily assignments. If you ever dare to err, you are punished, which seems to electrocute you enough to live in a semi-permanent fear of ever messing up again.

"To fail is shame inducing and painful, as the right ventro-lateral pre-frontal cortex is firing off all sorts of pain signals and the cortisol levels are rising," Dr. Swart explains. "Shame is one of the five basic human emotions that fall into the "avoidance" category – you will do anything not to feel like this."

As a result, perhaps you operate on a cocktail of adrenalin, anxiety and perfectionism, which is only reinforced by your colleagues, bosses, and firms. There are fewer places that seem to embrace the fixed mindset more than the corporate law firms of cities like London and New York.

These ecosystems are dominated by 'thinking' modes as opposed to 'feeling' modes – it's often amazing to me how disconnected many of the lawyers in our Escape community can be from their own bodies, as they've learned to switch off their emotional side. Becoming more robotic only strengthens the ability to perform, function, and achieve, while feelings might simply slow them down.

Many of them get an itch to start their own businesses. Yet after being a corporate employee for years, the very mindset that has served them well within the system – 'do what you're told, don't make mistakes' – is the exact mindset that can hold them back when they then try to break out on their own.

THE GROWTH MINDSET
On the opposite end of the spectrum are the startup entrepreneurs who spend their days playing around with code, ping-pong, big ideas and whiteboards. They are driven by passion, vision, and the desire to use their lives to create something larger than themselves. Tapping into their emotional side only helps their ability to stay motivated when resources are tight and dreams are big.

Dr Swart explains that Type 2 or Growth mindsets fear losing out on opportunities: "Type 2 mindset people would feel ashamed if they sat on the side lines whilst someone else ran off with a great idea. The way they work, gold nuggets emerge as 'aha' moments of insight that guide towards step changes in innovation."

For a person with a growth mindset, "failure is not bad and it can even be exciting."

To develop an innovative mindset, she talks about the importance of learning to combine "empathy for the context of a problem, creativity in the generation of insights and solutions and rationality to analyse and fit solutions to the context."

Improving the art of combining empathy, creativity, and rationality seems to be a skill that can only be honed through multiple experiments and failures.

My most successful entrepreneurial friends have at least one or two projects or business ideas that they've tanked along the way – these failures led them to sharpening their startup intelligence, personal resilience, and creativity. Like any other kind of art, it can take a hundred drafts to get to the good stuff.

"GOODBYE CAREER, HELLO SUCCESS"

I see the Escape mindset as one in which those who have thrived in fixed mindset environments start to embrace growth mindsets. Somebody who demonstrates this is Randy Komisar.

He holds a B.A. degree in economics from Brown University and a J.D. from Harvard Law School. He is also a founding director of TiVo and an entrepreneurship lecturer at Stanford University. While he now works at investment firm Kleiner Perkins Caufield & Byers, earlier in his career he served as CEO for LucasArts Entertainment and Crystal Dynamics, and acted as a "virtual CEO" for such companies as WebTV and GlobalGiving. Randy was also senior counsel for Apple Computer, following a stint in private practice, where he focused on technology law.

In my mind, his life has always been an example of the following idea, which he outlines himself in one of my favourite essays ("Goodbye Career, Hello Success"):

"When you lump together career goals and personal goals to get life, you are certain to find at first that day-to-day existence is more confusing. It's definitely easier to compartmentalise, to do whatever it takes to get the money at work and make excuses later to your family and friends. "After all, it's only business. I'm not really like that," you say. But over time, I've also discovered that when you stop distinguishing between work life and personal life, you stop caring about a lot of things that used to seem so important—like the title on your business card. At the beginning, that feels frightening—and humbling, too. But it also feels authentic. Better yet, it feels sustainable. I'm 45 years old now, and I feel as if, finally, I don't have to survive solely on adrenaline, speed, and agility. I can just follow one passion—one job—to the next and call it life."

Komisar's professional trajectory exemplifies the protean career – he took jobs that made him happy and sparked his passions. He focused on psychological success as opposed to climbing a pre-determined ladder. He built a nontraditional career path and created his own definition of success, by following a growth mindset.

GROWTH MINDSETS IN PRACTICE

The growth mindset is encouraged, Dr Swart says, by "re-igniting that curious childhood spirit that can get squelched by formal education and corporate life." While this might be easier said than done, I found some advice by Marc Eck, an American fashion designer and entrepreneur who turned a $5,000 investment into a billion dollar fashion and lifestyle company, particularly helpful. It will be helpful when considering how to transition from a fixed mindset where failure is feared at all costs, to a growth mindset where failure is a necessary and useful component

"I can tell you... that success doesn't look like an 'A+'. And failure isn't as simple as an 'F'. Failure could be very grey. You might arrive at an event in your life where you think, 'Wow I've succeeded,' and be getting the affirmation from all these outside forces, but if it's not aligned authentically to who you are, it can very much feel like failure," he says.

He rebrands the art of making mistakes with his observation that "success is merely the hangover of failure."

"I think we're taught in the system that failure is something that you should be ashamed of. Failure is for the dumb kids. You get an 'F'. You get a 'D'. You didn't comply. You didn't create the evidence of your worthiness," he says.

Failure, he argues, is a crucial element in building a unique learning atmosphere for yourself: more failures lead to more lessons that lead to more success.

An escape from a corporate law job doesn't have to mean an escape from the legal industry. The following stories relate to the concept introduced by Rikke a few chapters

---

back about not changing profession, just changing context. Some decided to stay in the law full-time but changed their roles or switched companies.

JOANNA'S STORY: "I STARTED A NICHE ONLINE PRACTICE"

My legal career started 20 years ago and as I entered a big City law firm as a junior lawyer, the long hours spent on multi-million pound deals that were part and parcel of the job were exciting. Then I met my husband and my first daughter came along.

Something in me changed and it was the hardest thing in the world leaving her with various nannies and nurseries. When my mum died shortly afterwards, I decided to stop and take stock.

Two years flew past, and my second daughter came along. Meanwhile the City law firms were mellowing and actually taking lawyers on a part-time basis. I found a role for three days a week. The girls were in a local nursery for those days too, so what could go wrong?

For starters, it was an hour to commute between the nursery and the office. The girls had to be dropped at dawn and collected at the last minute. I felt so guilty and invariably I shed a tear as I left them.

Then the firm started to moan and tut when I left the office even though I had done a full day. The work piled up and I was effectively doing five days of work in three days and even that wasn't good enough. I resorted to borrowing one of my daughters' scooters so that I could shave even more time off my commute and got quite a few odd looks as I flew across Waterloo Bridge in my pinstripe suit!

Gradually I started to get more and more anxious and unhappy; I hated leaving the girls in the first place. The moment I got to the office, I had this awful sinking feeling in my stomach as I fretted whether I would get through the work load in time.

The final crunch was when one day I got a call from the nursery to say that one of the girls was ill and I was to come back right away. I naively thought my boss would understand being a woman too. How wrong I was!

As I asked for permission to leave early, she completely lost her cool and exclaimed, "This is ridiculous, I don't go rushing home every time my horse is ill!" There ensued a stand up row with her on the difference between a horse and a child and I then burst into tears and fled.

The scooter and I jumped in a cab and I poured my heart out to the poor old cab driver and it was then that I decided to change my life. Whilst I loved being a lawyer, I loved being a mum too. Surely the two could work side by side. I resolved that they should.

I resigned needless to say and decided to set up on my own. I would work on my terms, even if it meant working odd hours such as from 9am until 3pm and then again in the evening when the girls were tucked up. I offered my services as a temporary lawyer to large companies to help them out in times of overload.

To my amazement, they were perfectly happy with my hours and were simply grateful for the extra help. And so my new business as a 'legal Mary Poppins' was founded and it has been going strong for seven years now.

Then three years ago I decided to start a niche, online practice dedicated to female entrepreneurs. I felt there were no lawyers who truly spoke their language and understood the juggling required in running a business and a family.

It even has an 'oven-ready' document shop that is open all hours and sells key templates that most start-ups need. I set up offtoseemylawyer.com.

Whilst it has been a very steep learning curve, I have loved every minute. I now have a team of 'family-juggling' lawyers who help me, all working from their own homes. Each day is different and all of my clients are always so full of excitement having taken the plunge to start their own businesses, it is a joy to work with them.

* * *

TIM'S STORY: "I STARTED TEMPLE BRIGHT"

I left for the usual reasons: long hours for relatively small financial reward, questions of meaning and a lack of autonomy. Leaving the big firm system was a gradual process. Having trained in a top ten firm in the City, I qualified in 1999 and stayed on for two and a half years.

By 2002 I'd had enough and I moved to Bristol, working at a big firm while I decided what to do. In 2004 I moved to a smaller firm to work with SME clients and I became a partner there in 2009. The next year I left and co-founded our own law firm Temple Bright in Bristol.

In March 2013 I moved back to London to run our second office, in Shoreditch just north of the City. So I've come almost full circle, but have managed to leave behind the aspects of City law I didn't like.

What I now have is that thing which people rightly want – autonomy. Moreover Temple Bright creates autonomy for all its lawyers, not just for the firm's founders.

Temple Bright was established in response to what my co-founder and I perceived as a failure of traditional law firms to meet the needs of entrepreneurs. Our approach is based on the four promises found on our website: City quality advice, reasonable and generally fixed fees, only senior lawyers, and responsiveness. We knew we couldn't keep these promises if we grew the firm along the traditional lines involving junior lawyers and gearing, so we developed a new law firm model.

We call this the "chambers practice": a solicitors' firm structured like a barristers' chambers. Our lawyers are self-employed, working in tight knit teams with a base at one of our two offices. We are emphatically not a "virtual" firm, with lawyers working from homes dotted around the country and little client-facing cohesion. Rather, we combine some aspects of that model (reduced overheads and autonomy for the lawyers) with aspects of the traditional firm at its best (a strong brand and unique selling propositions, sector expertise, physical offices).

The firm maintains the high standards of our City background but within an informal, supportive culture. Our lawyers generally earn more than they did in traditional firms, while working shorter hours and only for the clients they choose. The work they do is a mixture of matters referred from the centre and instructions won through their own marketing. Most find it easy to market themselves and Temple Bright owing to the firm's compelling message.

Since starting the firm in 2010 we have grown to over 30 lawyers spread across our two offices. We have over a thousand clients, ranging from startups to public limited companies. We won Bristol Law Society's "Regional Law Firm of the Year Award" in 2012, beating well established national firms in the process. This concluded our initial phase of growth in Bristol and gave us the confidence to open our second office, in Shoreditch in the heart of London's "Tech City".

My disengagement from City law was sealed at a particular moment in 2001. Having fallen asleep for a few minutes over the documents I was checking, I woke at 5am in a pool of saliva (mine). I soldiered on but later that day resolved that I would avoid being in this situation ever again. The move to Bristol and successive firms before Temple Bright now look like a planned route by which I took control; but of course that's only with the benefit of hindsight.

Moving to the Bristol big firm was easy because it was the world I knew, i.e. big law firms. Moving to the smaller firm was easy because I had the skills and by then I knew Bristol. Setting up Temple Bright was easy because, by then, my co-founder Justyn and I had lots of contacts. So no conscious preparation was necessary at any stage. However, if anyone had told me that morning in 2001 that within a decade I'd be starting a firm and then moving back to London to launch an office half a mile up the road, I'd have said they were crazy.

We started Temple Bright with a small injection of capital. Law is a cash business and if you have work for which you can bill at month end, funds should start to appear quickly and you should not need to borrow. We haven't taken any outside investment or loans to date.

I had some lawyer friends who had set up firms and friends who had run other businesses, all of whom gave useful advice. But the most valuable conversation partner has always been my co-founder Justyn. We tend to agree while often coming at things from quite different angles.

Often when I talked about leaving the law, people from outside the profession would point out that I'd worked hard to gain a well regarded qualification and some useful and lucrative skills. They encouraged me to find another way of using these skills without quitting. Following this humdrum but grounded advice was what finally led to Temple Bright.

Through my own choice I've taken on the demanding task of leading our London office. I don't work all night but I do work hard, and I have to live away from my home in Bristol. But what's oppressive in big firms isn't long hours, it is lack of control. Now if I'm tired I'll take the afternoon off and wander north through Hoxton and Islington with a book. If clients' expectations are unreasonable I'll tell them, or I'll ensure that I'm paid to go the extra mile.

Our model gives all our lawyers the same level of autonomy. We trust them to do a great job for clients and they are rewarded in proportion to their efforts. We don't bother with the extra rules or politics which usually exist in the traditional firm.

My life now is much better than it was as a big firm lawyer and I'll never go back.

* * *

IN A NUTSHELL

» A fixed mindset is one that is fearful of making mistakes. A growth mindset does not see failure as bad and thinks it can even be exciting.

» The growth mindset is encouraged by re-igniting the curious childhood spirit that can get squelched by formal education and corporate life.

» Some people do not escape law entirely but instead alter their professional context. Some decided to stay in the law full-time but changed their roles, switched companies, or started their own.

FURTHER RESOURCES

» Komisar, Randy. "Goodbye Career, Hello Success." *Harvard Business Review.* 1 Mar. 2000. Web. 10 Nov. 2014 <https://hbr.org/2000/03/goodbye-career-hello-success>

» Swart, Tara. *Neuroscience For Leadership: Harnessing The Brain Gain Advantage (The Neuroscience Of Business).* Palgrave Macmillan, 2015.

» Dweck, Carol. *Mindset: The New Psychology of Success.* Ballantine Books, 2007. Print.

EXERCISES

» Think of a situation where having a fixed mindset has helped you. Now think of a situation where a growth mindset has helped you. Explore how a fixed mindset would not have helped in a situation that called for a growth mindset.

» If you had a year left to live but still had to work through the year, would you be doing what you are doing today? If the answer is 'no', what would you be working on instead? Outline an ideal project that you would love to work on (as opposed to attempting to map an entire alternative career).

HOW I ESCAPED:
ANNABELLE'S STORY

"In the end, you just have to surround yourself with people who believe in you and avoid or ignore the people who don't."

I left the law because I wasn't happy as a lawyer. From the first class the first day of law school, I knew I didn't like it. But everyone told me that law school was different from being a lawyer – and that if I stuck with it I would see the practice was much more interesting.

After law school I did my three-year internship at the Brussels bar, mostly working in criminal and immigration law. It was much more interesting than law school, but it still didn't feel right. I grew more and more frustrated over time. I was often going to court to defend people who had committed minor infractions, while all around us there were these huge environmental problems growing worse every day. When you start reading about climate change, defending people accused of marijuana possession just seems kind of silly.

Of course not every case is small, but even on the big cases I felt like my clients reached me at the end of a long journey where so much had already gone wrong in their lives. I wanted to have a job that was earlier on in the process where I could actually have an impact on my clients' lives, rather than being the last step on a long journey, where I could actually do very little for them.

The moment when I knew I had to leave the law came during a particular case, in a small town. My client was of

African descent and was accused of having killed someone who had lived his whole life in the community. The victim's family packed the hall.

Needless to say, we didn't get the fairest hearing. I was exhausted after that, and my husband told me to take a break and not work for one night. I went to a local independent cinema and saw the movie *Happy Go Lucky* and laughed and laughed. I walked out of that movie theater knowing that I would stop as soon as my three years were up.

My husband and I had already been dreaming about travelling around the world for a few years. After that horrible hearing, we started planning our trip seriously. We planned out a route; we counted our pennies and figured out ways to save more money (we lived simply – no car, no new clothes, no expensive hobby, no big vacations, etc). We bought two bicycles and gear and we booked our plane tickets for Kenya. I think it's important not to plan too much or else you'll never do it. At some point you just have to jump.

In Belgium, pro bono legal work is reimbursed by the state at a fixed rate. But the state is so poorly organised that it takes them two years to pay you. So by working a lot of pro bono cases, I wound up receiving income during our first two years on the road. And then add to that that travelling by bike is cheap, we were sleeping in a tent or couch surfing and cooking our own food. You can travel cheaply if you want.

A month after I quit my job, my husband and I were riding bikes in Kenya. We spent 16 months cycling through eastern and southern Africa, visiting 12 countries and covering over 12,000 km. On the way we visited small farms and permaculture projects to learn more about organic farming. We had planned to bike around the world doing that, but then after Africa we felt that same need to do something positive, and so we traded our bikes for a video camera and traveled from New York to Rio by bus, making short documentary films about grassroots environmental initiatives that we found along the way.

That was a real shift in our project, and the real birth of the Permacyclists Project. It was another crazy 16 months, we had to teach ourselves how to make movies, how to get people to watch them, and all the while we were spending hours a day on the bus, living our lives in Spanish. But we made it to Rio for the Rio+20 summit, one of our films was screened at SXSW, and we were featured in a documentary on German public television, so we feel like it was a pretty good success.

We used to joke on the road that every day we biked was a day of my law career that was erased. But I think my law career did teach me a lot that was useful during our travels. The ability to speak publicly with ease, to meet new people and feel comfortable, to summarise complicated experiences in simple texts on the website. All of that I learned at the Bar.

I never really felt like a lawyer, it always felt forced. I enjoy taking risks and trying new things.

But I think that the drive to perfection that is so typical in lawyers hindered me. When we were making movies and working on our website, it was definitely hard for me to accept that it wouldn't be perfect because we were on the road and we didn't have the time to double check everything and make it as nice as we wanted.

Before we set out on our project, there were two camps when it came to the general attitude of friends and family. The first said, "Awesome!" They wanted to come along and encouraged us every step of the way.

The second camp were those who said, "You're an idiot!" They told me I was wasting my career and education, that we would surely be eaten by lions, that we would regret it, that I would never find another job.

In the end, you just have to surround yourself with people who believe in you and avoid or ignore the people who don't. Life is too short to let those people in.

I always dreamed of travelling the world. I have always loved reading books and learning new languages – the combination makes travel very appealing. I have to admit though, I secretly still feel like I haven't traveled the world! My husband makes fun of me, but I can't help but think of all the countries I've never been to. I don't think I'll ever stop travelling; there will always be somewhere new to explore.

The best advice I got was: Do it. Just go. Most of the time that type of advice came from people who were much older than me. I knew then that I was doing the right thing. I have never regretted my decision to leave, not for a second.

After our three-year trip we moved back to Belgium while I applied for my green card (my husband is American). In the mean time I took a small job as a paralegal to earn some money, and my husband and I had a baby. In September 2013, we moved to the US and now we live in the Catskills in New York State. Here, I'm taking care of our son while working as a freelance translator and helping out in a B&B next door.

Next year, I will go back to school to get a Masters in Environmental Policy and Sustainability Management at The New School in New York City. With that, I will definitely turn the page on my law career. Part of the reason that it appeals to me to be taking care of my son full time right now is that I spent a few years working like a crazy person. I know what it's like to not see your family and I don't want that anymore. I think the workaholic tendency is hard to shake – even during our trip we tended to work more than we should have.

For me to get here and live this life so many people have inspired me, so many books and films as well. I got the courage to bike by following the travels of other cyclists online and meeting them in person.

Travelling we met inspiring people every day. Everywhere we went we met people who were doing incredible things with so many fewer opportunities and resources than we have. It inspired us to keep track of what is important in life and to keep things in perspective.

* * *

[8]

FINAL THOUGHTS

"Only when we are brave enough to explore the darkness will we discover the infinite power of our light."

–Brené Brown

Before we finish, I wanted to mention a TED talk featuring relationship therapist Esther Perel. She talks about the unrealistic burden we tend to place on marriage (or long-term romantic partnerships) in a day and age where one person is suddenly expected to fill two opposing needs – our need for safety as well as our need for desire:

"We come to one person and we basically are asking them to give us what once an entire village used to provide. Give me belonging, give me identity, give me continuity, but give me transcendence and mystery and awe all in one. Give me comfort, give me edge. Give me novelty, give me familiarity. Give me predictability, give me surprise."

She discusses the couple's challenge to keep intimacy alive as they get further into the territory of the familiar (where apparently, desire goes to die). It resonated with me because it links to the parallels I have noticed with the relationship that many millennials try to build with their careers.

Perel discusses how marriage used to be a contractual agreement – we'll share property, we'll share kids, we'll share a social status. Nowadays, it has shifted: the person you marry is expected to still remain your partner in all those things, but they are also expected to be your family and fantasy and anchor and adventure all at once.

Similarly, a job used to be a long-term arrangement whereby you provided skills and your employer provided compensation for said skills – end of story. Today's workplace seems to be much more than just a marketplace. For millennials, 'work' has almost taken on a spiritual obligation – it has become a place where we are meant to find meaning and redeem not only ourselves but also the world around us.

As I've mentioned, through my work with Escape the City, I watched hundreds of high achievers go through the complex process of career change. Their intelligence, which had served them so well up until this point, often caused them to second-guess their intuition and rationalise away the feeling that they were on the wrong career path.

The conversations I had with members often mirrored the dichotomy that Perel discusses ("I want adventure, but also give me security"). I often met the lawyer who hits pause to spend six months volunteering in Uganda, the banker who yearns to transition into start-ups, and the advertising executive who moonlights with his food blog.

Their day jobs feed their need for comfort and security and the adventures they dabble in feed their need for transcendence and exploration. To try and reconcile the two into a single job seems to be a similar exercise to building a marriage where a partner is a best friend as well as an erotic fantasy. Possible -- yes. A given? Not necessarily.

It is hard – if not impossible – to (immediately) generate a generous salary from volunteering, starting a business, or a blog. I meet a lot of high achievers who suddenly morph into anti-careerists.

However, a regular income is also necessary to survival. To deny that is to live in an adolescent fantasy world, and the question that often trips up a lot of Escape members is how to translate their fantasies into a reality that pays the rent. They want a meaningful job, but what if they don't want to give up their quality of life? They want the freedom of running a business but how can they do it without the risk? They want to switch industries but can they do it without starting at the bottom all over again?

The struggle often dissipates when we apply the same reality check that Perel applies to relationships: our day jobs were never meant to be the singular, primary source of meaning in our lives. Where one finds meaning is a deeply personal and unique matrix. While a job can strengthen self-esteem or provide a sense of belonging to an industry or field, it was never meant to replace endorphins, the loyalty of close friends, intimacy, laughing until your stomach cramps, or the feeling of gazing into a starry night sky.

Perhaps we are meant to have hobbies and passions that never translate into full-time jobs (at least not straight away). We have multiple selves within us. Some are lucky enough to reconcile the playful self and the working self into one role – others have a job in order to pay the rent and their true fulfillment comes from family, friends, and passions outside of their day job. To place too much pressure on our job to provide us with fulfillment that it was never meant to provide can overshadow the opportunity to find meaning in a range of activities and relationships.

Having said all this, I am not arguing that we should give up on the idea of love – if anything, I am a firm believer and fighter *for* love – for finding work you love. My point is that love is a journey that is made much easier when expectations are realistic.

By no means am I underestimating the powerful clarity that can come with feeling like you've found your mission, but in my mind, that is a different thing to a day job. They're related, but it's like true love and long-lasting marriage – one does not necessarily imply the other. And just like in a romantic relationship, the less pressure we put on a day job to live up to unrealistic expectations, the more we become able to enjoy it for what it is, rather than what we wish it could be.

Then again, there is a difference between not being passionate about your day job, and being downright miserable. If your job is costing you more than it's giving you, it might be time to consider alternative options.

I hope that this book has provided you with some ideas on how to do so.

We began by looking at how the career choices that our generation faces are more complex than those of our predecessors and so we are likely to face an impasse more frequently than our parents did. An impasse is a learning opportunity through which we can update how we interact with the world.

We then excavated the psychological barriers that might be preventing you from even allowing yourself to wander off the path. The mindset of a lawyer can provide its own unique cocktail of fears and anxieties.

Thirdly we saw how coaches can be useful in helping you to find alignment within yourself as you embark upon marrying your values with your day-to-day work.

We explored resistance and self-sabotage. The best way through this is through experimenting strategically, as your comfort zone expands the more that you do things that scare you.

The financial aspect of transition was also addressed – often lawyers used their existing skills to find flexible, paid work within the legal industry as they embarked upon their transition.

We also looked at how the fixed mindset fears making mistakes while the growth mindset is encouraged by reigniting the curious childhood spirit, where failure is not inherently bad (and can even be exciting) – provoking renewal.

Finally, I wanted to leave you with the end of Sam's story as well as a few more stories. I also wanted to share the main lesson I took away from writing this book, which is best summarized by researcher Brené Brown:

"Owning our story can be hard but not nearly as difficult as spending our lives running from it. Embracing our vulnerabilities is risky but not nearly as dangerous as giving up on love and belonging and joy—the experiences that make us the most vulnerable. Only when we are brave enough to explore the darkness will we discover the infinite power of our light."

Finding work you love is not always a smooth journey. But I sincerely hope that this book might have made your next step a little easier, whatever that step might be.

SAM'S STORY (CONT'D):
"NO RISK, NO REWARD"

I knew that I would never reach the very top as a corporate lawyer: I lacked the passion and drive to do so. No doubt I could coast along doing what was necessary and ticking all the right boxes as a cog in the machine. But what sense of achievement would I get from coasting? I aspire to way more than that. I want to be creating things, building products that I'm passionate about, working on projects that I believe in. I want to be able to point to tangible successes. I want to be a winner. And the way I felt was that I wouldn't ever truly be a winner or think of myself as a success when what I was doing was a chore. How do you summon up the drive and commitment necessary to really make the most of your potential when you have no passion for what you're doing?

When you look at examples of people who have really made the most of their potential, invariably they are people who have really loved what they do. People like Michael Jordan, Kobe Bryant and Lebron James are winners: they are three of the greatest basketball players of all time. And what do they have in common? They all love basketball. They want to be playing, they want to be working hard to improve and they want to be chasing success in their sport. Allen Iverson was a great player, unquestionably one of the best of his generation. But he wasn't much of a fan of practicing (Youtube his press conference – it's a classic). And guess what, in terms of achievement, he doesn't come close to the others.

You can make a similar argument in tennis. Roger Federer and Rafa Nadal are real winners, both having achieved phenomenal success throughout their careers. Between them they've won 30 Grand Slams. They could both have quit years ago, but they love what they do. The passion and drive that this engenders inspires them to consistently achieve great things. In contrast, Andre Agassi was a superb player – a first-class talent. But he didn't win on the same scale as those guys and he has publicly stated his hatred for the sport: "I play tennis for a living even though I hate tennis, hate it with a dark and secret passion and always have."

Agassi famously tanked games in the nineties, and who knows how much he would have achieved if he had had the same desire as the likes of Federer and Nadal. For Agassi, tennis was simply something that he did, and was capable of doing, very, very well. He didn't love it and it didn't inspire him.

That's how I felt about working in a law firm. It was just something that I did. And I can't expect to achieve really great things in something that I'm not passionate about. I don't mean just having success, just being impressive. I want to be really, really good at what I do. I want to be the absolute elite, right at the top. And that would never have happened for me in law, because I would never have been able to call on the drive and passion required to do so.

Aim high, and then aim higher. No risk, no reward.

After leaving the law, I focused on re-tooling and testing my theories about what I actually wanted to do. I needed to re-engage skills that had become stagnant during my time as a lawyer, but most importantly I needed to discover what else was out there.

You can plan and research as much as you like, but you won't really know if you're suited to something until you give it a go. My time as a lawyer had taught me that at least. So I went out and tried new things.

After Escape, I worked for a Canadian payments start-up, defining its marketing strategy and re-positioning the brand for launch in Europe. Soon I was combining this with building partnerships, sales calls and content marketing.

I went from law to partnerships and PR, with dalliances in sales and operations, and detours to marketing, content production and web design. All in three months. And it hasn't really stopped.

Having made the break from law, it quickly became very clear to me that I could go as far as I was willing to take myself. When you put yourself out there, opportunities come to you. When you reach out to new people and take an interest in new things, you realise time and time again just what possible career paths are available to you. My professional life now is a far cry from what it was a year ago.

I have learned significantly more in the past nine months than I did in all of my time working in law. But let's not forget, I have earned significantly less – that fact is inescapable. For me, the trade-off is well worth it. Why? Firstly, because I now know with complete clarity what I want to do with my life, and secondly, because I now have the opportunity to go ahead and do it.

For the past few months, I have been building WeJaunt.com, a platform for finding and booking carefree weekend breaks for young professionals. I'm working all hours, but nowadays I'm more than happy to do so.

As well as providing exclusive trips for pre-existing groups of friends or colleagues, we also match individuals and small groups with new people to Jaunt with. Because of this, I'm often talking to people in the City and in corporate jobs, many of them lawyers. I hear all of the same complaints that I was spouting this time last year. The great thing is that I don't have any of those complaints anymore.

A year ago I was clock-watching, checking documents that likely no one would ever read and wondering how I had ended up quite so disillusioned with my career after all of the study and hard work – a lawyer with zero interest in the law.

Now I spend my days mocking up iOS apps, filming marketing videos and coordinating trips that really excite the people coming on them. It's all a phenomenal thrill.

The difference in my mind-set and motivation is seismic, but the thing that underpins this change is fundamentally very simple: I'm trying to get something off the ground that I really believe in; something that I really, passionately, give a shit about.

Professionally, I'm in a completely different world. And the greatest trick the law ever pulled was convincing so many people that this world didn't exist.

If you've had a similar experience or are looking to make the break from the law, I'd love to hear from you. To get in touch with me, find me on twitter @sambo_hall or drop me an email at sam@wejaunt.com.

* * *

A FEW MORE STORIES

HOW I ESCAPED: ALISON'S STORY

My partner and I are both very keen skiers and love the mountains, so without knowing exactly where it was leading, we decided to start investigating ways in which we might be able to turn our passion into a career.

The first step for me was to "do a season" in the French Alps. This was something I had always wished I had done when I was younger, so I signed up with a tour operator to be a "Resort Rep" for the winter season and left my job at Simmons & Simmons.

And so I found myself posted to Serre Chevalier Vallée in the southern French Alps. I spent the season organising holidays, solving guests' problems and, of course, skiing and absolutely loved it.

I have a confession: I have not fully left City law! During the winter season we are based in Serre Chevalier Vallée full time. During the off season and summer months I have been able to find contract work with City law firms and/or with the City law industry.

It became clear to me during my first season that I was not ready to fully give up my City law knowledge and experience and we discussed how it would be possible for me to maintain my connection with the legal industry and also keep my legal practising certificate current.

This had a number of advantages, including: (i) keeping up to date with contacts in London for marketing purposes; (ii) allowing me to continue to advise the company on legal issues; and (iii) providing me with the possibility of going back to law in the future.

I am currently completing a contract as a professional support lawyer which nicely pulls together my experience of the legal industry and my experience of launching a new product.

My partner and I launched Chez Serre Chevalier in 2011 as a tour operator providing ski, snowboard and summer holidays to the resort of Serre Chevalier Vallée in the French Alps. We both left City jobs to set up and run the company, which is now a well-established and rapidly growing business.

We identified Serre Chevalier Vallée as offering something new and set out to offer innovative packages, not just following the standard "cookie cutter" holiday. We are passionate about enabling as many people as possible to have the opportunity to enjoy the mountains and with this in mind we developed a flexible service where anything is possible from a simple self-catered apartment to a full service luxury chalet, so there are options suitable for all.

Being professional and friendly in everything that we do is the cornerstone of our business. This runs through the entire process from initial holiday enquiry, to sorting out the finer details and then during a guest's stay in resort. Without a doubt, these are qualities which have become second nature to us thanks to our City backgrounds.

Our approach appears to have paid off as we have been shortlisted for a World Snow Award in the Best Specialist Tour Operator category!

We financed the move away from law through a combination of using savings and my partner and I doing contract work in the off-season. We are lucky that we have not used any debt finance at this stage.

Setting up the business has been a very demanding task, but my legal background has been a huge advantage. From setting up a limited company and deciding on the structure of the business, to discussing both UK and French VAT issues with our accountant and reviewing contracts (in both English and French!), we would have struggled without my legal training.

There is also a whole myriad of rules and regulations specific to the holiday industry that we have to be aware of and abide by. My professional experience means I have the knowledge and skills to navigate these issues.

My time as a lawyer has also provided me with very useful transferable skills such as the confidence to negotiate contract terms and how to work in a team and deliver excellent customer service.

We were extremely careful with each step we took in leaving City jobs and setting up the company that we minimised any risk – from both a personal and business perspective. As mentioned below, we set up the business piece by piece and have expanded very gradually and have been very careful not to take on any work that we will not be able to do to the best of our ability.

One of our main inspirations was the team at Go-Montgenevre. Go-Montgenevre is an independent tour operator in the neighbouring resort of Montgenèvre that prides itself on its community values and willingness to help other small businesses in the area. The best advice we received was from Go-Montgenevre: "Don't run before you can walk." We set up the business piece by piece and have expanded slowly and surely over the past three years.

Before we set up the business and we were debating our future options, it quickly became clear that we shared their values of wanting to run a successful business that was able to create excellent value holidays, individually tailored to the needs of our customers. They were, and continue to be, a great source of support and information for us and they were instrumental in helping us to build our business.

From a more personal perspective, another person I try to emulate is Nick Cronkshaw who is Head of Corporate Tax at Simmons & Simmons. In particular, in the way he built and maintained an incredibly loyal and hard-working team whilst always being very approachable and maintaining a good sense of humor.

Obviously Jackie (my partner's cousin who had been diagnosed with terminal cancer) remains a huge inspiration to us both.

The general attitude of friends and family was overall very supportive if a bit bemused. People kept telling us we were "very brave", but to us it was simply the logical next step towards finding out whether we could turn our mountain dream into a reality.

When we are out skiing on a Monday morning and the sun is shining then it all seems rather amazing. However, when it's 5am and minus 26 degrees Celsius and I'm struggling to put the snow chains on our minibus I do sometimes wonder. There are always advantages and disadvantages to a job and, for me personally, the advantages of our current set up far outweigh the disadvantages.

I miss the corporate tax team at Simmons & Simmons. I was born and bred at Simmons and miss the daily banter and camaraderie of the team. That said, we now run their annual ski trip so I still see some of them on the mountain!

If you are thinking about it, you should do it. This is for two reasons: (i) pretty much any experience you gain outside the law will have relevant transferable skills so you can always go back to the law if you want to (this in itself demonstrates that I have not lost my risk averse nature!); and (b) if you don't do it, wouldn't you always wonder "what if?"

* * *

HOW I ESCAPED: VIDU'S STORY

I didn't enjoy the Legal Practice Course and within hours of starting my first day as a trainee, I knew that this wasn't the career for me. I entered law with the idea (like many) that I would do it for a few years and then move in to what I wanted to do.

If I look back, the fundamental mistake I made is that I didn't think about what I wanted to do as a job at university – my priorities at university were more about having fun, playing sport and getting through my degree with the least amount of work possible. Combining this with the fact I applied for jobs in 2007 when the hiring market was much more liquid than today meant that I found myself with some great training contracts at the end of my second year at university.

At the time, this was a complete no-brainer to accept – someone was going to pay me a great salary to do a prestigious job that I had lined up before I left university – I felt that I had successfully achieved what I had entered university to do but I was fundamentally missing the point. I should have been focused on learning from leading academics, having a great time and discovering more about what I truly enjoyed in terms of work/career. Like many people, I was too focused on the vanity metrics – namely my degree grade and perceived prestige of the job I had on exiting university!

I was fortunate to end up in the private equity team at Linklaters and was sent on secondment to a great private equity fund – I saw there what the job entailed and had an epiphany. The job the deal teams did was really interesting to me – it stood at the cross functions of entrepreneurship and finance. I realised, however, that what really interested me was actually building a business from scratch and whilst a career in investing would move me closer to that end, fundamentally the only way I could achieve what I really wanted out of my career was actually starting a business myself.

The biggest barrier to leaving was the perceived financial opportunity cost of future earnings as a lawyer.

I was very lucky to be working for a brilliant partner at a great firm. I was getting great career development opportunities and doing work that, within the spectrum of legal work, did interest me. Why would I throw away a position like that?

I also believed that I did have the tools to achieve high levels of success in a legal career (if I applied myself) and reap the benefits that come with this (money, prestige and a more interesting job at the senior levels). I also thought about what I had invested – a degree, LPC and four years of working hard at developing my skills as a corporate lawyer.

I think what is most telling is that, I had a great legal career – it couldn't have been going better – and I still decided to leave it because it wasn't moving me towards my long term goal of starting my own successful business.

Finances are a big concern. There were a couple of things I did and am doing to stay afloat financially:

SAVE
I didn't do enough of this, but I had some money in the bank, which kept me going for a while.

NETWORK
You have met lots of people in your legal career – can you help them and get some money in return?

Reach out to people, offer them something of value – build on your old relationships with people, as they already know your name and background – you'll be amazed at how this can pay off (see the next point!).

GET ANOTHER JOB

I got a job working part time doing sales at a startup – however, this company ran into financial difficulty and I was in and out within four weeks. I am shortly starting a role at a venture capital fund doing lead generation, which will cover my expenses.

This is a brilliant opportunity as the work I will be doing has a lot of crossover to what I need to be doing in my business right now (i.e. finding customers) and I will be working with really smart people who can teach me skills relevant to my career as an entrepreneur.

This opportunity came about through my old client network. There will be a way for you to use your legal skills to earn money – whether this is for a small company, doing "pseudo-legal" work (i.e. more admin type legal work), paralegal work etc – you should be willing to do anything if it pays!

The question you have to weigh up here is how much time can you dedicate to earning money vs. your core activity of starting a business as a job will distract you. What's ideal is if you can find a way to work in a field that develops relevant skills or has some crossover with your job.

GENERATE REVENUE FROM YOUR BUSINESS

If you're starting a business, generating revenue early solves two problems – 1) it validates that people will pay for what you have to offer and 2) you can use this revenue to live off or cover your business costs. Unless your business is creating a new market, is a technologically novel solution or is in the life sciences field, this is generally possible and can stop you investing too much in the wrong idea as well as help your personal finances.

LIVE CHEAPLY

When you earn, you spend (generally). You have to accept you will have to cut out some of the things you did before to make your money go further. This is a balancing act. I live very cheaply now – I eat out far less, don't buy new stuff and don't really go on holiday etc. This can be really tough but you have to accept this is the drawback of giving up money from a job that you don't like.

It's a question of setting your priorities – personally, this means that I don't really drink and spend money on big nights out like I used to, but I still spend money on going on dates with my fiancée, and still go out with mates but don't drink (which also means I can get up without a hangover, get work done and make better use of the gym membership I'm still paying for!).

If you plan and are disciplined with your spending, your quality of life won't drop – you'll just find out what really matters to you.

The best thing about leaving the law is that now I'm doing something that feels right.

What this means tangibly is that I'm working towards a goal that I want to head towards – I wake up daily knowing my efforts are applied in taking me towards a career that I want. The worst thing about being in law was that I felt that I was working hard towards an outcome I didn't want (put very simply, why on earth was I working all hours of the day on becoming a great lawyer if I didn't want to be a great lawyer!).

It's also great developing new and relevant skills. I have learnt how to code reasonably well, I am learning more about what "digital marketing" actually means, sales, product development etc – all skills I need and were not being developed in my legal career.

The personal effect of all of this is that fundamentally I am a lot happier! It's as simple as this – whatever you want from your life and career, if being a lawyer isn't helping you get there, why are you doing it?

* * *

HOW I ESCAPED:
ALISON N.'S STORY

I gave up law just over a year ago. Since then, I have spent half my time in Ghana and Uganda, training staff, overseeing projects, visiting communities. The rest of the time has been in the UK fundraising, doing back office work, supervising the African teams remotely.

When I originally went out alone to Africa I had read a book about an American hairdresser who went out on a whim to Kabul to set up a beauty school. I remember at the time thinking that was such a great thing to do – and why couldn't I do something similar. As lawyers I think it is very easy to get stuck on a kind of career conveyor belt. So it is always good to look at people who have made different choices.

Five years ago I founded Lively Minds, a small development charity, to help improve the lives of children living in poverty in Ghana and Uganda. I initially gave up my job for a year to live in Africa and start the charity.

I then returned to the UK and went back to law. I ran Lively Minds alongside my job as a Government lawyer for four years (I worked as a lawyer four days a week, and for Lively Minds one day per week and in my annual leave and weekends). But eventually it became clear that the charity needed to grow and this required a full-time CEO. So I gave up the law to run Lively Minds in September 2012.

Lively Minds works in the poorest and most remote rural villages in Ghana and Uganda, where children do not get the most basic opportunities in their early years.

We have three training programmes that reach children at a crucial stage in their development, enhancing their education, health and wellbeing. So far we have already given over 23,000 children in 65 communities a chance for a brighter future.

It started to get to a point where I felt that Lively Minds was holding back my legal career. I felt unable to apply for positions as they would not be compatible with the charity work. I also realised that although I found the law very stimulating – it was not where my passion lay. I used to be on the tube every day wishing that I was headed somewhere else. Eventually I got a lucky break when a funder offered to pay half of my salary costs for two years. That gave me the safety net to leave the law and commit fully to Lively Minds.

I already knew what my role at Lively Minds would involve. And I had half of my salary covered in advance. So I did have a safety net. But I also had to just trust my instincts and jump.

I was given some salary costs from a funder. But I had to make a big salary sacrifice. I had to move out of my flat and rent it out. Fortunately I have been living in Africa for half my time, where it is cheap. Next year is going to be a big financial squeeze, but overall it is definitely worth it.

I spoke to the trustees of the charity, to make sure that they agreed with my decision to work for the charity full time. Once the funding was in place, I then handed in my notice.

I think my legal skills helped in three main ways. First, the problem-solving skills as a lawyer have held me in very good stead. This enabled me to analyse the situation, separate the root causes from the symptoms, assess risk and create practical strategies to address these issues. Second, working for a charity requires very good governance. My legal experience has helped me with all the necessary administration, compliance, paperwork, grant writing side of things.

Finally, my work as an advisory lawyer has helped me to train staff and beneficiaries. The discipline of explaining the issue in simple terms, setting out options and making recommendations has been key for Lively Minds, as our work is about empowering people to make their own choices and changes.

When I first set up Lively Minds my friends and family thought I was crazy. But over time they have seen it take over my life – and I think they mainly felt it was inevitable that I would give up the law to work for Lively Minds full time.

I am good friends with a couple who gave up work, fixed a tent on the roof of their car and went travelling round the world for two years. Their advice to me was "One life, live it". Where you are fortunate enough to be in a position to be able to follow your passions and dreams, I think it is a mistake not to do so.

* * *

HOW I ESCAPED: MARTIN'S STORY

I had always been concerned that I had made a poor choice when I chose a career in law. It turns out choosing a profession based on an obsession with the film A Few Good Men was rather rash. I was largely unhappy – despite being reasonably successful in my field – I knew that it wasn't what I wanted to do.

In short, I didn't enjoy the work, the hours or the people. When the opportunity arose to leave my firm and the industry, I grabbed it.

I had certainly thought, many times, 'What am I doing this for?' but I don't think there was any real epiphany that I recall. I was just aware that I was unhappy.

The opportunity to leave was rather suddenly upon me and so I didn't prepare as much as I should have done – hence the hasty decision to focus on what started out as a hobby/distraction.

The Corner Theatre (TCT) was only ever meant to be something on the side – a bit of fun. I wanted to do something creative that was completely at odds with a day job that I perceived as intolerable. The Corner Theatre was about t-shirts, street wear and doing something different. I design everything, source the ethical tees and have them printed locally using eco-ethical processes.

I had some savings and dipped into them to help set up TCT which was otherwise bootstrapped.

I spoke about my decision to leave with my wife. If anything, she convinced me to do it because she knew I was miserable and therefore much less fun to be around. She is always supportive. I'm incredibly lucky.

My family and friends were more shocked than anything. I think I am identified as a 'lawyer' and so jumping into an unfamiliar territory such as fashion was always going to confound and astound. Generally, however, they have been cautiously optimistic though I feel they're always wondering when I'm going to start taking life seriously again.

The best advisors are other entrepreneurs who have taken the leap too. Also, no one knows what they're on about – everyone is bullshitting about something.

The preparation for setting up TCT (all those practicalities like setting up a company, bank account etc) took up far more time than I wanted – mainly because I wanted to spend all of it drawing new things, testing fabrics and sweet talking printers. I also spent quite a bit of time being patronised by a developer (who must hate me still for being so dense). After launch, it was about marketing – calling/emailing contacts offering up samples and generally schmoozing, talking to potential stockists (Top Shop was on the cards for a short while) and sorting/posting any orders. Even the admin was fun though.

After about a year of TCT, my wife and I found out we were expecting a baby and the reality of needing a steady income hit home. As such, I reluctantly turned back to law – though now I work in-house at an NGO. The hours are fantastic, though the pay is considerably worse. At this point in my life, I am happy with that balance to let me see my family and work on TCT (and other side-projects).

Is there anything that I miss about City law? The money was always good. Also those free meals after 7pm – the pad thai was never a disappointment. But I have a better work/life balance now – in-house at an NGO means very regular and reasonable hours. I'm home in time to pick up my daughter from nursery and generally able to see my wife for goofing off.

My parents (and their parents) are entrepreneurs – they have run a restaurant in Thornton Heath (the Bunga Raya) for over 30 years. My dad once told me that I would have to run my own business one day as he was convinced I couldn't take orders... I think it was a compliment.

* * *

HOW I ESCAPED: CONNOR'S STORY

I was a corporate lawyer for three years. It took a momentous event to finally make me move on and when I did I found myself adventuring in the Montana wilderness. With the space to stretch my legs and brain (in between the fishing, camping and backpacking), I was able to focus on figuring out what I wanted to do. Somehow I found the perfect job and jumped on the opportunity. I feel very lucky to have just started as the programme manager for Lightning Lab – the first digital startup accelerator to be based in Auckland, New Zealand.

Before I escaped I was a corporate lawyer (read in the voice of a person introducing themselves at an AA meeting). I flew through University at warp speed, worked on my career in summer breaks, got the dream clerkship at a big firm, never looked back. But. About six months after I started as a grad, deep down I think I knew that the life wasn't for me. I felt uninspired. There wasn't that knot in my stomach telling me that I was on the cusp of something that would change my life, there was just the next day. The same thing. The same desk. The same coffee and suit.

I consulted for and helped out startups and friends working on new projects in my spare time and I have been subscribed to Escape the City for a few years. So that should give you a fair indication of where my heart was. I, however, am a tenacious fellow, and I wasn't going to give up on my job easily. I knew that I was learning invaluable lessons, meeting the right people, that it wasn't the right time... blah, blah, blah. The same old excuses.

So I did the corporate law thing for three years and, truth be told, I actually don't regret it. Because I did learn some great things and meet some incredible people. But I think that I can only say I don't regret it now that I am out.

For me, it was always going to be hard to leave the comforts of a secure job in law. I liked the life I had built up, I liked the people who I was hanging out with and I liked the (limited) time I was spending out of the office. And there is the thought that when you leave a job, who knows which aspects of your life will change.

Then my mum got sick. She lives in the US and I hadn't seen her in a few years. So there was only one option open to me. I quit my job and moved to Bozeman, Montana. At that stage I knew that I wanted to leave law and do something else, but I didn't have the guts. I find it hard to admit that it took a huge event like my mum getting sick to finally force me to move on.

While helping out with mum (who eventually made a full recovery), I did a lot of thinking, quite a bit of fishing and even helped a new friend renovate his house. As my mum got better my girlfriend (who also quit her job in law and came over) and I spent time exploring and adventuring around the epic Montana wilderness.

Once my head was clear, I was able to sit down and decide which direction to go in. I looked at what I enjoyed doing, which was consulting and bouncing ideas around with startups, and tried to find a job that incorporated those things.

It turns out that a role just like that had opened up with Lightning Lab, the first digital startup accelerator to be based in Auckland, New Zealand. I was hired as their programme manager, and we are now building up to a three-month accelerator programme which kicks off in March next year. That means that our days are filled with marketing (media, social media and actually talking to real humans) and managing the nationwide tour of events that started with our launch last week.

Behind the scenes we are raising private capital and sponsorship to run the programme as well as locking in high profile mentors and generating interest in the Angel and VC investment circles. To say I'm enjoying this new position is an understatement.

When reflecting on this career change and my "escape", there are some difficult parts of the transition. As you may expect, there is a pay cut associated with escaping. But as you must also expect, I am not doing this for the money. In my new role, I'm really happy and I feel like I have made the right choices.

* * *

HOW I ESCAPED: EVA'S STORY

I got a scholarship to do postgraduate studies in photography that paid for my fees and a monthly allowance. My MA studies helped me to focus on a specific project: Traces Within. Since 2008 it has been internationally recognised through awards and exhibitions and at some point it will be published. After finishing the MA I decided to try studying cinematography at Ealing Studios and Art Therapy at British Association of Art Therapists.

I enjoyed that a lot. And then I started my teaching training. I now deliver international workshops and in 2013 I was invited as a global expert from ISSP to facilitate a self-portrait workshop in Latvia which is part of a bigger project linked to Riga 2014 Cultural Capital of Europe. You can see more in my blog evavoutsaki.blogspot.com and website evavoutsaki.com

I left the law because I was born to become who I am: an artist and an educator. I don't see photography as a career. It is more like breathing; it comes very natural to me.

The turning point was in 2003, after having a workshop with Anders Petersen, a living legend of contemporary photography. He told me I am talented so that gave me lots of responsibility to follow that path. His presence was mesmerising.

In terms of preparation, I applied and gave exams for a scholarship to do an MA in photography and once I took it I moved to England. In the meantime and for the next year or so I kept working as a lawyer when in Greece.

The truth is that I was always occupying myself with photography, having exhibitions, delivering workshops. I was also teaching Turkish and translating/interpreting for many years. I guess what happened is that I started doing photography full time.

I financed the move with bits of savings, the scholarship and lots of work. As a law leaver you need to adjust your needs and learn how to sometimes survive on less. But with a big smile...

Everyone was expecting my move...Or at least those who knew me. But I guess that the person who supported me more was my best friend Katerina. I still remember our conversation when she told me: just do it!

My family still dreams of me going back to law, deep within them. But at the same time they recognise that doing what I really love keeps me happy. So, this matters to them.

The best advice I've received was possibly from my aunt Demeter: do what you really love. And from Anders Petersen: don't be afraid to do it. They may sound clichéd but at that point I needed to hear these advices.

At some point I was angry at myself: why I didn't quit law from the very beginning, from the first day at university? But then I realised that my path was meant to be that way and that all this emotional struggle made me stronger and truer to myself.

ACKNOWLEDGEMENTS

This book almost remained forever dormant on my laptop. Katherine McDonald contacted me out of the blue and it is thanks to her that you are reading this right now. I could not be more grateful for her help. Special thanks also to my brother for being my biggest cheerleader.

I'm grateful to the early readers who were kind enough to shape this: Ian Hutchinson, Alfonso Giuliani, Janine Esbrand, Emma Wilson, John Sheehy, Natalie Speranza, Alison Howarth, and numerous other Escape members who wished to remain anonymous.

The contributors who were generous enough to share their journeys: Mark Hosking, Annabelle Vinois, Jim Brough, Alison Dickie, Henry Burkitt, Deanne Cunningham, Tim Summers, Vidu Shanmugarajah, Alison Naftalin, Susanne Skoruppa, Hannah Needham, Eva Voutsaki, Martin Ngwong, Emma Mapp, Amber Hoffman, Scott Margetts, Pete Dowds, and Daniel van Binsbergen. Special thanks to Sam Hall for his excellent writing.

Rachael Armitage and Michelle Chan, for their assistance in the early stages, and Ivan Cruz for his beautiful design.

Joanna Penn, Rob Archer and Charly Cox, for the constant inspiration.

Rob, Dom, and Mikey, for being brave enough to start Escape the City and brilliant enough to grow it to what it is today. The Escape family is something very special and I feel privileged to be part of it.

I also feel privileged to have my parents and brother, who are three of my closest friends, as well as my chosen family of friends who are scattered around the globe. A massive thanks to everyone who encouraged me to keep writing, especially when I felt silly about doing so.

REFERENCES

Archer, Rob. "Career Paralysis - Five Reasons Why Our Brains Get Stuck Making Career Decisions." *Slide Share.* 4 Sept. 2010. Web. 16 Nov. 2014. http://www.slideshare. net/robarcher/career-paralysis-pt-1-five-reasons-why-our-brains-get-stuck-making-career-decisions-5128274/

Berman, Casey. "The First Step in Leaving Law Behind – It's the Money, Stupid." *Above the Law.* 18 Jan. 2013. Web. 10 Jan. 2015 <http://abovethelaw.com/career-files/the-first-step-in-leaving-law-behind-its-the-money-stupid/>

Bolton, Phil. "How To Get Focused And Find Fulfilling Work" *Less Ordinary Living.* 21 Sept. 2011. Web. 10 Nov. 2014. <http://www.lessordinaryliving.com/blog/how-to-get-focused-and-find-fulfilling-work/>

Brown, Brene. *The Gifts of Imperfection: Let Go of Who You Think You're Supposed to Be and Embrace Who You Are.* Hazelden, 2010. Print.

Brene Brown. Web. <brenebrown.com>

Butler, Timothy. Getting Unstuck: A Guide to Discovering Your Next Career Path. Harvard Business Review, 2009. Print.

Butler, Timothy. "Working with Symbolic Intelligence: The 100 Jobs Exercise." Harvard Business School Exercise 812-064, December 2011.

Career On Your Terms. Web <http://www.careeronyourterms.com>

Charly Cox. Web <http://charlycox.com/readytoshine.html>

Clarke, Marilyn. "Plodders, Pragmatists, Visionaries and Opportunists: Career Patterns and Employability." Career Development International, 14.1 (2009): 8-28. Print.

Clarke, Marilyn. "Understanding And Managing Employability In Changing Career Contexts." *Journal of European Industrial Training,* 32.4 (2008): 258-284

Crane, Ethan. "How Can I Make The Escape From My Career Less Terrifying?" *Escape The City.* 1 Feb 2015. Web. 5 Mar. 2015. <http://www.escapethecity.org/blog/get-unstuck/can-make-escape-career-less-terrifying>

Csikszentmihalyi, Mihaly. *Flow: The Psychology of Optimal Experience.* Harper Perennial Modern Classics, 2008. Print.

Coyle, Daniel. *The Talent Code: Greatness Isn't Born. It Is Grown.* Arrow, 2010. Print.

D'Souza, Steven. *Not Knowing: The Art of Turning Uncertainty into Possibility.* LID Publishing Inc, 2014. Print.

de Botton, Alain. *The Pleasures and Sorrows of Work.* Vintage, 2010. Print.

Dweck, Carol. *Mindset: The New Psychology of Success.* Ballantine Books, 2007. Print.

Deresiewicz, William. "What Are You Going to Do With That?" *The Chronicle of Higher Education.* 3 Oct.

2010. Web. 1 Nov. 2014. < http://chronicle.com/article/
What-Are-You-Going-to-Do-With/124651/>

Esbrand, Janine. "Not Knowing: The Art Of Turning
Uncertainty Into Opportunity". Escape The City. 1 Dec.
2014. Web. 10 Mar. 2015. <http://www.escapethecity.org/
blog/exciting-opportunities/notes-night-knowing-art-
turning-uncertainty-opportunity>

"Escape the City – The Escape School."
Eventbrite. Web. <http://www.eventbrite.co.uk/o/
escape-the-city-the-escape-school-1711682488>

Escape the City. "The Money Question." *The Escape
Manifesto: Quit Your Corporate Job – Do Something Different!*
Capstone, 2013. Print.

Eventbrite. Web. < https://www.eventbrite.co.uk/>

Gerber, Michael E. *The E-Myth Revisited: Why Most
Small Businesses Don't Work And What To Do About It.*
HarperCollins, 1995. Print.

Hall, D T. "Protean Career, Definition(s) of." Work and
Family Researchers Network. 18 Sept. 2011. Web. 1 Dec.
2014. <https://workfamily.sas.upenn.edu/glossary/p/
protean-career-definitions>

Hall, Sam. "Is It Worth Being Unhappy in Your
Profession?" *Escape the City.* 26 Mar. 2014. Web. 10 Nov.
2014. <http://www.escapethecity.org/blog/get-unstuck/
worth-unhappy-profession>

Hansen, Rikki. *"Career Change: How Do You Start?"* Online
Video. Youtube. 22 May. 2013. <https://www.youtube.com/
watch?v=5XnNlRwOezQ>

Ibarra, Herminia. *Working Identity: Unconventional Strategies for Reinventing Your Career.* Harvard Business School, 2003. Print.

JP Morgan Jr. Web <http://jpmorganjr.com/>

Komisar, Randy. "Goodbye Career, Hello Success." Harvard Business Review 1 Mar. 2000. Web. 10 Nov. 2014 https://hbr.org/2000/03/goodbye-career-hello-success

Lagace, Martha. "Feeling Stuck? Getting Past Impasse." *Harvard Business School Working Knowledge.* 25 Apr. 2007. Web. 10 Nov. 2014. <http://hbswk.hbs.edu/item/5548.html/>

Legal Nomads. Web <legalnomads.com>

Less Ordinary Living. Web < http://www.lessordinaryliving.com/>

Lewin, K. "Frontiers in group dynamics. Concept, method and reality in social science; social equilibria." *Human Relations,* 1947, 1, 5-40

Meagher, Michelle. "About." *Worker Bee Free.* 24 Dec. 2013. Web. 20 Dec. 2014. https://workerbeefree.wordpress.com/about/

Meetup. Web. <http://www.meetup.com/>

Morgan, John. "*How To Find Your Passion*" Online Video. Youtube. 19 Jun. 2011. https://www.youtube.com/watch?v=5XnNlRwOezQ

Kate Northrup. Web. <www.katenorthrup.com>

Parker, Monica. *The (Un)happy Lawyer. A Roadmap to Finding Meaningful Work Outside of the Law.* Sphinx Publishing, 2008. Print.

Pink, Daniel. *Drive: The Surprising Truth About What Motivates Us*. Riverhead, 2011. Print.

Pendry, Jane. "How to Explain the 'Next Steps', When the 'Next Steps' are Unknown." *Escape The City*. 1 Jan. 2015. Web. 4 Mar. 2015. <http://www.escapethecity.org/blog/exciting-opportunities/explain-next-steps-next-steps-unknown>

Pressfield, Steven. *The War of Art: Break Through the Blocks and Win Your Inner Creative Battles*. Black Irish Entertainment LLC, 2012. Print.

Pressfield, Steven. *Do the Work: Overcome Resistance and Get Out of Your Own Way*. Black Irish Entertainment LLC, 2015. Print.

Pryor, Lisa. *The Pin Striped Prison*. Picador Australia, 2008. Print.

Ritter, Devo. "What to Do When You Don't Want to Be a Lawyer Anymore." *The Muse*. 21 Mar. 2014. Web. 9 June 2015. <https://www.themuse.com/advice/life-after-law-what-to-do-when-you-dont-want-to-be-a-lawyer-anymore>

Robin, Vicki, Joe Dominguez, and Monique Tilford. *Your Money or Your Life: 9 Steps to Transforming Your Relationship with Money and Achieving Financial Independence: Revised and Updated for the 21st Century*. Penguin, 2008. Print.

Saville, Margot. "The Pinstriped Prison." Sydney Morning Herald. 19 Sept. 2008. Web. 10 Nov. 2014.< http://www.smh.com.au/news/entertainment/books/book-reviews/the-pinstriped-prison/2008/09/19/1221331197568.html?page=fullpage#contentSwap1>

Seligman, Martin. *Authentic Happiness: Using the New Positive Psychology to Realize Your Potential for Lasting Fulfillment.* Simon & Schuster Australia, 2002. Print.

Sethi, Ramit. *I Will Teach You To Be Rich.* Workman Publishing Company, 2009. Print.

Shin, Laura. "How Sam Polk, Former Wall Street Trader And 'Wealth Addict,' Broke Free Of His Golden Handcuffs". *Forbes.* 2 Mar. 2014. Web. 14 Feb. 2015. <http://www.forbes.com/sites/laurashin/2014/02/03/how-sam-polk-former-wall-street-trader-and-wealth-addict-broke-free-of-his-golden-handcuffs/>

Swart, Tara. *Neuroscience For Leadership: Harnessing The Brain Gain Advantage (The Neuroscience Of Business).* Palgrave Macmillan, 2015.

The Career Psychologist. Web <http://www.thecareerpsychologist.com/>

Trinetti, Matt. "How Can I Land My Dream Job?" Escape The City. 1 Jan. 2015. Web. 7 Mar. 2015. <http://www.escapethecity.org/blog/exciting-opportunities/how-can-i-land-my-dream-job>

16399268R00129

Printed in Great Britain
by Amazon